BIG SMOKE
BIG SCREEN

20 Film Writers on London & Cinema

A WeLoveCinema Book

Big Smoke, Big Screen: 20 Film Writers on London & Cinema

Copyright © Walloh Limited, 2024

https://we-love-cinema.com/

First published 2024 by Walloh Limited

ISBN 978-1-0685560-0-5

Edited by Tom Barnard

Typeset by Elaine Miles

Cover design by Rejane Dal Bello

A CIP catalogue record for this book is available from the British Library.

"It is difficult to speak adequately or justly of London.
It is not a pleasant place; it is not agreeable, or cheerful,
or easy, or exempt from reproach. It is only magnificent."

– Henry James

CONTENTS

I FIRST FELL FOR LONDON THROUGH A SCREEN. BEFORE I WENT TO THE CITY FOR REAL, I WENT THERE UNDER THE GUIDANCE OF AN ANIMATION DEPARTMENT LOCATED 5,432 MILES AWAY IN BURBANK, CALIFORNIA, SITTING CROSS-LEGGED ON THE CARPET OF MY NAN'S LIVING ROOM FLOOR WITH MY FACE PRESSED UP AGAINST THE TV.

I was just four years old when *The Great Mouse Detective* (retitled *Basil the Great Mouse Detective* for UK audiences) came out on VHS, years after its original 1986 theatrical release in the US. In hindsight, it might have been the first film I ever saw. It's the sort of statement that feels true, even if it isn't, since none of the other movies of the period lingered quite as strongly in my impressionable child brain as *Basil*'s depiction of the rainy, fog-covered Victorian metropolis; the sewer-centred chase sequences; the rousing score by Henry Mancini; the epic finale that literally takes place on the clock face of Big Ben.

What I couldn't quite get my head around was that London was a real place – a short ride away, as my Nan would point out, just thirty minutes by train. Like Basil, you could actually go there. Only you'd be taller. Or you'd expect to be.

In hindsight, *The Great Mouse Detective* harnesses a not-so-subtle metaphor, of course, though one I'd never considered until I recently revisited the film in preparation for this book: London is a city that, by design, has a habit of making you feel small. Not merely by the standards of its vast, daunting size, but through the indifference it has towards those who choose to spend their lives there. In London, be prepared to be swallowed whole or sucked down a drainpipe – man or mouse, it makes very little difference.

But the film also can't help – or has no choice? – but to relish the romantic nature of the great city, too. It draws up all the bad stuff we tend to associate with big city life – traffic, sewage, violence, permanent risk of things falling on your head – and puts them in conversation with the city's insurmountable literary history; a sense of scale and wonder; the meeting point between grit and grandeur; a rousing belief that this is a place where things *really happen.*

I, like so many who call it home, have fallen in and out of love with London more times than I can count. But I wonder whether it's possible to have any other relationship with this city that truly makes sense. One minute, the noise and the speed at which it moves can prove alienating; the next you're enamoured with its winding passageways, its myriad of people from all walks of life.

I often find myself staring into the abyss of an overpriced pint, hearing the yells of the pub's patrons as a waitress drops a glass, wondering: Do I love London because I love London, or *because* I am a Londoner? If you live here, though, it is customary that once a week you must declare that you've had enough, that you are moving to Lisbon, actually, or somewhere equally warm, friendly, slow, and forgiving.

A recent visit to a remote part of Europe prompted me to examine what makes a city valuable on a personal level. Yes, the weather is almost always better anywhere else, the trains probably run on time, and there's a lot less smog than in The Big Smoke (the nickname, for those who don't know, hails from the city's reputation as a cesspit of pollution in the 19th century – nice!). But you mean I have to travel two and a half hours by bus, and then train, just to catch the latest Spielberg movie? And then *back* again?

Aside from the obvious draws, like living in proximity to the people who matter, I quickly realised the most important thing to me about living anywhere is... access to a cinema. The moment I'm not near one, I begin to feel disconnected, cut off. In a world as complicated as this one, that might seem trivial; ridiculous, even. But we have to take the things we love where we can get them, or what's the point?

I don't just mean the local Odeon, with its sticky carpets and a general sense of having had better days, but a place dense with repertory pleasures – a town that celebrates the history and weight of films and filmmakers from all over the world and treats them and their work with respect. In a city like London, where it's easy to be overwhelmed, the notion of quality cinema access makes proper sense. Because the cinema is, in itself, a place where we go to get out; a doorway to destinations far-flung – and London's cinemas provide a hell of a lot of doors. For me, cinema's

main appeal has always been to pacify a desperate, never-ending sense of wanderlust by allowing me to drop into Istanbul, or South Korea, or a small town in Belgium I'd never heard of before at the drop of a hat.

For those who live life as something to discover, London is home to great, vibrant picturehouses of all shapes and sizes, with more than 100 screens spread across the capital, pulsating like little hearts, sending cultural shockwaves into the map of the city. Knowing I am close to these institutions, I sleep a lot better at night.

It's the variety that stands out. As I sit to write this introduction, a quick Google search tells me that it's possible to start the day with a screening of *La dolce vita* at the Ciné Lumière at 1pm, before moving on to David Byrne's musical comedy *True Stories* at the Prince Charles at 4:15pm; I could then step out into the bustle of Chinatown, grab something to eat, and still have time to make it for Robert Altman's *3 Women* at the Close-Up Cinema at 8pm, before hopping on a 20-minute bus up to the Rio in Dalston, where they have an 11pm-till-late "holiday from hell" double bill of *The Descent* and *Tourist*

Trap, courtesy of horror film club Category H.

That's an opportunity, and a privilege, that Londoners often take for granted, and a gift that so many cinephiles scattered across the country would give their right arm to have on their doorstep.

This idea was what was crucial to our mission at WeLoveCinema, the website where I proudly worked as editor between 2018–2023 (and through the bulk of a COVID outbreak, when cinemas were closed). The simple goal behind our site was to make it easy for hungry audiences to plug themselves into London's often overwhelming cinema scene; not just using our nifty search function, but by covering a more diverse array of films than most publications, big and small, and bringing attention to what was out there whether you were a casual fan or a dedicated cinephile. I genuinely think we succeeded in doing that, even if our time was sadly cut short.

Which brings us to this, our book, *Big Smoke, Big Screen*. As one era came to a close, we wanted to mark the occasion and encapsulate the two things that made our site possible: a love of London, and a devout passion for the big screen experience. The essays, written by the site's frequent contributors (and a handful of new ones), those living within London, on the outside, or some version of both, draw lines between a love of the big screen and the city itself, often finding that passion through the lens of a personal connection.

When putting this book together, I asked the contributors what London and cinema meant to them, and as you'd imagine the response produced a wide range of opinions and styles. The resulting essays are frequently charming, sometimes rambling, thrillingly tangential, but all refreshingly honest in approach.

What I appreciate most about these writings, though, is their attempt to merge place and memory with a powerful sense of cinephilia. To find meaning in interactions with the cityscape, and to dig out the overlap in celluloid dreams and the streets. They are not all pro-London (how truthful would that be?), but they each find something to appreciate about the city – a sense of community, a sacred place to take refuge, an acknowledgement of how a film or filmmaker contributed to their love of the medium. London is, after all, a compromise – but you hope at the end of the day it all feels worth it.

What emerges throughout, I think, are valuable ruminations on how films themselves have the power to inform the places that we choose to inhabit, and how we wield the movies in our daily lives as artefacts worth more than just mere entertainment – as guides to living and growing, as tools for grappling with who we were, who we are now, and who we would like to be.

Throughout the book, we've also recommended 200 films – classics, curios, hidden gems – which taken together paint a huge, varied portrait of a city that has and always will defy easy classification. London can so often feel represented in only two ways on screen: romantic wonderland, or gangster's playground. Many of the recommendations here fill in the gaps, showcasing the city in lesser-seen ways, exposing neighbourhoods and underrepresented communities that have always been integral to the city's real identity.

London is not, and never has been, the romantic playing field of Paris on celluloid; nor, like New York, is it the place where plucky go-getters with good hair head to make their dreams come true. No, what London offers is constant reinvention; it stops you in your tracks before you can make anything permanent of it. But as these essays show, the city is always willing to announce itself in new and interesting ways, across a million different stories.

And just like London, the essays collected here offer an eclectic mix of perspectives and expression: musings on people, places, filmographies, hopes, dreams, histories, disappointments – sometimes all at once. If London is, indeed, a city of smoke, I hope these writings help to clear the view a little. •

BACKSTAGE AT THE PRINCE CHARLES

BY HANNAH STRONG

Tarantino called it London's "queen's jewel." Friedkin called it a "shithole." Whether you've sat through seven hours of *Sátántangó* or a Nic Cage all-nighter, the Prince Charles is a clarion call to the city's most devoted cinephiles

A few days into 2022, streets still icy and the London air still crisp, an excited audience settled in for the long haul. 11 and a half hours of viewing, to be exact – excluding two intervals to refuel and glimpse daylight. This is how long it takes to watch the Extended Editions of Peter Jackson's *The Lord of the Rings* movies, back-to-back, which I know because I've done it twice now in the basement screen of the Prince Charles Cinema.

A giddy audience turned out for this annual tradition, which memorably included one patron yelling "Yes, we all know he broke his foot!" at the bit in *The Two Towers* where Viggo Mortensen spontaneously kicks a helmet in a moment of rage. Then, at the end of the third film, *The Return of the King*, as Frodo, Bilbo, and Gandalf set sail to Valinor, I found myself crying – something I do a lot when watching films, admittedly, though never before at a movie in this franchise. Yet on this occasion, the collective experience – the act of watching these films I love so big and so bright on the screen – prompted an emotional reaction. The laughter and genuine joy of this event have stayed with me since, but it's just one example of what marks central London's premiere repertory cinema as the beloved institution that it is today.

Nestled between the bustling restaurants of Chinatown and the heinous Leicester Square M&M's Store, you have to weave your way through tourists posing for photos among Soho's rabbit warren of streets to find it, though you can't miss the illuminated marquee. The Prince Charles Cinema opened on the 26th of December 1962 – though originally, "Cinema" was "Theatre" and the building was intended as a new addition to the capital's West End. Perhaps due to the saturated market, the theatre soon opted for a different crowd and rebranded as a porn cinema, where it would show films including Just Jaeckin's *Emmanuelle* and Tinto Brass's *Caligula*. The building has operated as a cinema ever since – the only independent cinema in London's West End – and is located just a stone's throw away from the Cineworld, Vue, and Odeon, which regularly host world premieres attended by A-Listers. When it comes to cinema love, though, you'd be hard-pressed to find the same passion and excitement anywhere else in the vicinity.

Day after day, an eclectic audience packs out the cinema's two screens, turning out in droves for everything from *The Sound of Music* singalongs to *In the Mood for Love* on 35mm (in fact, Wong Kar-wai's seminal romantic drama has played at the Prince Charles every single week since the cinema reopened following its long closure during the pandemic). Its shabby-chic interior and wide-ranging programme – plus glowing endorsements from the likes of Paul Thomas Anderson, Quentin Tarantino, and John Waters (who, at the time of writing, stars in their pre-show "turn your phone off" video) – have positioned the place as a sort of mecca for movie lovers in London, bridging the gap between new releases and repertory cinema, showing a pleasing mix of canon classics, underseen gems, and films you didn't even know existed.

Upon entering the main auditorium of the Prince Charles for the first time, it's impossible not to notice its rather unique layout. The "satellite dish" curve to the floor means you sit at a slight upward angle facing the screen, giving a sense of drama to every showing. This can be a bit annoying if you end up seated behind a particularly tall person, but for the most part it's a charming detail that sets the cinema apart from its multiplex neighbours. In 2008, the balcony of the main space was converted into a second screen, allowing the cinema to show twice as many films. With 300 seats downstairs and 104 upstairs, it's big enough that a packed house feels like an event, but small enough that seeing a film there still retains an intimate feel.

I know the Prince Charles like the back of my hand. In the nine years I've lived in London, it's become one of my most important places, the site of countless discoveries and memorable first watches. When I first moved to London I didn't really know anyone aside from a few university friends, so I spent a lot of time at the cinema, and the comparative cheapness of the tickets compared to other London venues was a draw before I had any idea how diverse and exciting the programming was – or came to know the incredible staff who bring the place to life. In cities I'd lived in previously, I'd loved independent cinemas for their warmth, and for showing films I couldn't find at my local multiplex, and the same relationship quickly formed with the Prince Charles. But it wasn't until I became a film journalist – and started making friends with people who shared my love of the building – that the place began to feel like a second home.

Part of the reason the Prince Charles feels so special to me is the community it fosters. The cinema has an active presence across X and Instagram, regularly tweeting trivia about the building's history and interacting with customers alongside providing programming information. If you tweet the Prince Charles an idea for a screening, it's as good as logging it on their massive suggestions chalkboard (located in the downstairs lobby). In 2018, I tweeted asking them to consider replicating a programming idea from Dublin's Light House Cinema, to show Luca Guadagnino's *Call Me by Your Name* and Jonathan Demme's *Stop Making Sense* as a double bill. The Prince Charles agreed it was a great idea and dutifully obliged. After several years of talking about it, in the autumn of 2023, the cinema managed to secure Miloš Forman's *Amadeus: The Director's Cut* for a 35mm run. Given that the film hadn't screened in the UK for many years, it represented something of a big win. Their willingness to respond to audience feedback and tailor their programming choices accordingly makes the Prince Charles feel like an oddly communal space – a cinema that, theoretically, anyone can have a hand in programming.

But there's a very real team of people behind the scenes who work tirelessly to bring the Prince Charles to life, from the cinema's hands-on, cinema-loving owner Gregory Lynn, to the crack team of customer assistants who scan tickets and serve popcorn. Paul Vickery has been a part of the Prince Charles family for 16 years. "I was an AD in TV commercials and music videos when I found out about the Prince Charles, and despite being born in London, living in Romford, I'd never heard of the place. People at film school even, they only talked about the BFI, the ICA, Curzon Soho. But I started going to the Prince Charles on my days off, because it was £1 in the afternoon. I just became an obsessed customer who went every day for the matinees – and I went so much, Chloe, who was the programmer at the time said,

'We've got some jobs going, why don't you just work here?'"

Having served as Head of Programming since 2011, Paul's job involves a fair amount of detective work, as rep cinema is often a case of tracking down the right person who can connect a cinema to the films they want to screen. It's not as simple as bunging on a DVD – especially when you have a discerning audience to think of. There are licenses to acquire, prints to locate, and crucially, sums to be done about viability. For a cinema that shows everything from second-run new releases to martial arts curios, plus a healthy dose of animated features, too, every film that makes it to the Prince Charles screen does so with a lot of thought and care.

This dedication has led to some extremely unique events. Films like Phil Tippett's stop motion opus *Mad God* and Kyle Edward Ball's viral sensation *Skinamarink* received exclusive UK runs at the Prince Charles, while "Worst Film in the World" *The Room* regularly sells out special screenings with director Tommy Wiseau in attendance. Brendan Fraser, Isabel Sandoval, and Andrew Garfield are among the stars who have graced the stage, and among the cinema's most beloved supporters was the late, great filmmaker William Friedkin, who came to the Prince Charles in 2017 for a screening of his once-maligned masterpiece *Sorcerer*. As Vickery tells it, "He walked in, looked around, boomed 'Look at this shithole!' and cracked up laughing." Friedkin's films have played at the cinema in heavy rotation for years; after he died in 2023, the cinema screened *To Live and Die in L.A.* in tribute to a packed house.

Edgar Wright and Christopher Nolan have been spotted among the punters (the latter was also instrumental in the cinema's acquisition of a 70mm projector), while ardent supporter Kevin Smith – who has appeared in-person at the cinema numerous times – has a toilet cubicle named in his honour, after he remarked it was unfair Tarantino had the bar named after him. In a city not lacking for ritzy film spaces, the Prince Charles is beloved for its quirks and lack of pretence. Dedicated cinephiles share the space with eager newcomers and intrigued tourists. In any given week the programme reflects its eclectic origins and ethos: you can roll straight out of a screening of *Shrek* and into a showing of *Gangs of New York*.

Making all of this happen is the projection team, led by Jamie Brooker. Alongside the rest of the projection team (Dan, Svein, Camille, and trainee Zuza), Jamie works on assembling and disassembling prints, operating Digital Cinema Packages, and problem-solving the myriad complications that can develop when projecting film on film. Tucked next to the second screen is the main auditorium's projection booth: a small strip of room where my attention is drawn to the massive 70mm *Interstellar* print sitting atop the film platter, ready for later. Without the archives or on-site storage of institutions such as the BFI or New York's Lincoln Center, the Prince Charles has a constant stream of prints coming and going, which all require assembly, checks, and disassembly when they're ready to go home. Considering film projection is something of a dying trade, the team at the Prince Charles are in high demand.

But with prints sourced from all over the world, sometimes there are unexpected problems – such as when the team attempted to show *Howard the Duck* in 2022. "The print arrived and had vinegar syndrome like you won't believe," Jamie tells me, refering to a process whereby the film strip chemically degrades, leaving a vinegar-like smell. "It stank, and I already had a bad feeling, but when we started to run it through the projector... the picture was terrible and the sound was warped. It was hard to even keep it steady on the projector. It was so bad I went downstairs and told everyone I'd try to keep going for a bit, but they'd probably be better off going home, as it was in bad condition. A few people stayed, but eventually, I had to stop it. It was killing me to try and show such a poor-quality print."

Most of the time, things go more according to plan. In fact, beyond the occasional focus adjustment at the start of a film and the tell-tale flicker on-screen, you might forget the projectionists are there at all, such is the nature of the job. They're the unsung heroes of the cinema experience, though to the cineastes who happily turn out to see Cassavetes and Kubrick playing on film, they're a vital component.

Also crucial to the Prince Charles' status as a beloved London cinema institution: their regular movie marathons, which vary in length and theme but always draw in crowds. Whether it's an *Evil Dead* all-nighter, a day packed with mystery movies that are only revealed when the opening credits roll, or a Disney-themed pyjama party, they offer something that audiences can usually only find when the latest blockbuster comes out a couple of times a year: a place to watch movies late into the night. In a capital beset by gentrification and the erosion of community spaces, London is becoming less and less of a 24-hour city; the Prince Charles is one of a handful of places outside of bars and clubs that runs all-night events.

On a few occasions, these marathons weren't even for movies. In 2010, the cinema screened all 121 episodes of hit television drama *Lost*. Over 100 guests took part in the marathon, which lasted from Monday 13th September until Friday 17th September – by the time the finale finished, only 21 were left standing (or sitting, to be more accurate). Among them was Danny Kelly, who recalls: "Upon leaving, I struggled over to HMV to buy the new Weezer album, which had just come out, and was coincidently titled *Hurley* after one of the show's characters and had a photo of him on the cover. Took it to the till in my sleep-deprived, kinda paranoid state. Staff member looks at the artwork, laughs, and asks – I kid you not – 'Have you ever seen *Lost* before?' Think I mustered up 'You have no idea,' and left." The success of the event was such that the cinema hosted another in 2017 to mark the end of HBO's *Game of Thrones*.

There are many such stories of how beloved the Prince Charles is among its patrons. In the process of researching this essay, I was inundated with anecdotes from people to whom the cinema has played a memorable role. Rory Doherty attended a screening of Jackie Chan's kung fu caper *Police Story* trilogy on September 8th 2023 – the day that Queen Elizabeth II passed away. "The first movie glitched in the climactic fight scene and the lights came up and a member of staff came to the microphone and said, 'Hey, sorry about the problem, we're fixing it now.

Oh, also, the Queen died.' That's how a lot of people in that room found out. But then the third film, *Supercop*, was made during Britain's colonial occupation of Hong Kong, and many people in the audience – myself included – didn't realise it starts with an extended full-frame close-up on a *massive* portrait of the Queen. I don't think we heard the dialogue for about a minute. People were too busy laughing and yelling."

Not all stories involve the death of a monarch, of course: Leah Bilson told me the cinema inspired her and two friends to create their own film club at the start of 2022. "We all got memberships and we've seen twenty new films so far (*Days of Heaven* was our last one) and it's been amazing fun. I think we've all discovered some new favourites and it's been a great way of making sure we spend time together when we're busy. I've fallen in love with the cinema since we've spent so much time there."

At the time of our talk, Paul tells me the Prince Charles just had its best year ever. Ticket sales are up, the range of films playing at the cinema is more diverse, and the audience's appetite for the collective theatrical experience show no signs of slowing down. As the streaming wars, Hollywood's recent shutdown over working conditions, and a glut of characterless big-budget movies laden with samey CGI all present a question mark over the future of cinema, the Prince Charles is a little beacon of hope nestled among the fusty alleyways of Soho. Proof that if you build it, they will come – old and young alike, from all walks of life, brought together by a passion for the big screen. •

LONDON DOCUMENTARIES

01 LONDON

1994 — dir. Patrick Keiller

A wandering, psycho-geographic grappling with our great city, narrated by legendary actor Paul Scofield.

02 FINISTERRE

2003 — dir. Paul Kelly, Kieran Evans

A kind of "city hymn" set over the course of 24 hours, with music by Saint Etienne from their album of the same name.

03 LONDON: THE MODERN BABYLON

2012 — dir. Julien Temple

Temple's vibrant, swirling, trance-like ode to The Big Smoke shows it as a creative force to be reckoned with.

04 NATIONAL GALLERY

2014 — dir. Frederick Wiseman

An exhaustive, three-hour-long (ahem) portrait, courtesy of cinema's most meticulous chronicler of institutions.

05 LONDON SYMPHONY

2017 — dir. Alex Barrett

Wonderfully wordless monochrome musing on the capital, set to a vivid score by James McWilliam.

08 RONNIE'S

2020 — dir. Oliver Murray

This spirited doc charts the life and legacy of Ronnie Scott, namesake of London's premier jazz club.

06 THE PONDS

2018 — dir. Patrick McLennan, Samuel Smith, Sue Turton

Wonderfully life-affirming and lo-fi dive into Hampstead Heath's community of dedicated pond dwellers.

07 THE STREET

2019 — dir. Zed Nelson

What happens to the locals when the craft beer shops move in? Eye-opening look at Hoxton mid-transformation.

09 IF THESE WALLS COULD SING

2022 — dir. Mary McCartney

Abbey Road is further immortalised in this enlightening backstage tour (courtesy of Paul McCartney's daughter).

10 SCALA!!!

2023 — dir. Jane Giles, Ali Catterall

Appropriately eccentric tribute to King's Cross' fallen grindhouse cinema, a bastion of the weird and wonderful.

THE SILVER TIPPLE

BY BEN FLANAGAN

A booze-soaked odyssey through London's cinematic drinking holes shows how two struggling institutions might need each other more than we think. Brave new world, or last orders?

orget the foyer: when the lights come up, I want to get the hell out of Dodge to discuss what I've just seen at the pub. Search "pub" on Google Maps (the only way to travel) and you'll get roughly 3,500 results in London alone. By comparison, there are around 100 cinemas. But it's about quality, not quantity – particularly with London institutions that are protected and fiercely fought over.

At the pub, notions of comfort and homeliness coincide with opportunities for revelry within the community (and shouldn't we say the same about our cinemas?). With their dark alcoves and attention to detail, pubs are the stuff of dreams: inviting bronze taps, disinterested old-timers reading the paper from a corner stool, incongruous artefacts left by a punter (perhaps an oar or a typewriter), green ceramic loo tiling, and packets of Tayto strung up like sausages. Pubs are an aesthetic paradise, and it's easier to consider the alchemy of filmmaking over a pint of plain than the dregs of a Tango Ice Blast.

On-screen, then, pubs have proven to be a fruitful location for filmmakers looking to explore the capital. There is great potential for mapping London onscreen through its pubs, too. In an ever-changing urban landscape, it's a vast project, but one that could also tell us where cinemas are and where they are going.

Ruminating on the potential connection between pints and projectors, I thought it best to begin my journey at my favourite cinematic pub, Camden's Mother Black Cap, one of many taverns to appear in that booze-sodden masterpiece *Withnail & I*. It's a novice's idea of a watering hole: a haunting, dilapidated, and dangerous point of potential violence. From my Peckham abode, I hop on the Thameslink and cross the city in minutes.

En route, the film floats back to me. Two young but destitute actors, Withnail (Richard E. Grant) and Marwood (Paul McGann), spend the first 20 minutes rolling around their flat, resorting to drinking lighter fluid when the booze runs out. In the pub, director Bruce Robinson switches to wide, deep focus shots. Modern life only makes sense in this one locale. That's not to say it's free from conflict. No sooner does Marwood, who has been resigned to cleaning Withnail's vomit from his boots with petunia oil, walk to the lavatory, than a large besuited man calls him a "ponce." Petrified! At the urinal, his anxious voice-over goes into overdrive when he spots the words "I FUCK ARSES" etched into the wall. "Who fucks arses? Maybe he fucks arses! Maybe he's written this in some moment of drunken sincerity! I'm in considerable danger here... I must get out of here at once."

That even the pub has lost a semblance of sanity is a key factor that drives the duo out of London and onto their eventual non-holiday. The setting of 1969 holds significance beyond just being when Robinson, who based the characters on his own circle, lived in his own cursed flatshare. There is the distinct air of something lost. The Beatles all but broken up; Harold Wilson's time in power drawing to a close; Murdoch acquiring *The Sun*.

These thoughts race through my mind as I reach Camden High Street. Asking a local bobby for directions, I learn my first lesson in Movie Magic: Mother Black Cap is not a real place. A portmanteau of local institutions The Black Cap and The Mother Red Cap... and yet the crumbling filming location sits two miles away, in Tavistock Crescent.

A quick Google tells me all this as I begrudgingly pay homage in Mother Red with a stiff drink. After, I hightail it to Westbourne Park, where I stumble upon the inevitable: The Crescent location is long demolished, whatever history it once housed replaced with a tedious concrete apartment block. At last I understand the evergreen meaning of *Withnail & I*: that London is always at the end of something special, and the start of something worse.

It's spitting now, so I march through Portobello Market with haste, looking for a good pit stop. Backstreet boozers are a common location in the films of Guy Ritchie, a marker of street cred and urban knowledge for the director as much as his characters. As such, they make a distinct signpost of gentrification, I think, now passing Westfield. In his first film, the Tarantino-fetish-caper *Lock, Stock and Two Smoking Barrels*, the pub is a near-constant location for dimly lit mischief and double-visioned miscommunication. In the "Samoan pub," which opts to serve umbrella cocktails in lieu of pints, Ritchie shoots in close, static shots as though the viewer is perched on a barstool, bleached light from below bouncing red from the sticky walls.

By the time we get to his latest geezer film, Ritchie seems to have forgotten the price of mead. *The Gentlemen*, from 2020, shows a clean London populated by as many Americans as Cockneys, with Matthew McConaughey's unconvincing mobster "king of the jungle" Mickey Pearson groan-inducingly ordering a pint and a pickled egg at a taproom so inauthentic you'd be surprised to realise it is in fact portrayed by Shepherd's Bush gastro-pub The Princess Victoria. I enter from the rain, and am saddened to learn that the pint Pearson drinks – "English Lore" Pale Ale from Ritchie's brewery – is not among the taps. This cinematic vision of the modern inn should be of no surprise to those who have set foot in Fitzrovia's Lore of the Land, the venue owned by Guy Ritchie since 2019. Ostensibly a proper boozer for proper people, it's a tourist trap for flat-capped stag-do-wells to visit from the home counties. London identity is malleable. Its size, along with its ethnic, cultural and economic diversity, not to mention its infinite history, means that anyone who wants to be "of the city" can be. But Ritchie's films are like someone with only faint memories of the place, attempting to package its every cliché to uncaring investors. I ask for a Madrí shandy, weight of the world suddenly on my shoulders.

It's easy to get existential about London when watching Ritchie's films, a despair only matched by Bob Hoskins' own in *The Long Good Friday*. This still razor-sharp '80s thriller depicts the laundering of organised crime through neoliberal Thatcherite politics, with Hoskins' wannabe reformed mobster courting American investment as a way to clean up the Docklands, and who finds himself unwittingly caught up with the IRA as he does so.

I wander Limehouse's often silent streets, where pubs appear to me like jump scares on every second corner. Hoskins' own slow and futile untangling of the web of information culminates in a moment of pure symbolism:

his pub, The Lion and Unicorn, is blown up. Director John Mackenzie barely shows us the place, just a shot of a long and nondescript Wapping street, at the end of which sits a tall, bright, and regal inn. Its destruction, a perfectly fine pub usurped by a rival in a show of power, proves a simple, elegant way to shove the East End's regeneration in the audience's face – one which will eventually lead to Canary Wharf and the significant start of Qatar's ownership of the capital.

This thing goes all the way to the top, in other words, which is why the pub on-screen – always different, but always the same – is such an important image to maintain. The pub as fortress is indeed a recurring motif of London cinema. In *Shaun of the Dead*, The Winchester is a place of greater safety – or so Shaun (Simon Pegg) hopes. I cross the river and head south, in search of the same. In the film's opening scene, Shaun's beloved local turns sour when his girlfriend dumps him by the slot machine. His connection to the space, lovingly shot with rich oak colours and twinkling liquor bottles, is a manifestation of his stunted refusal of adult responsibility. Writer-director Edgar Wright ironises this when the zombie apocalypse happens the next day, and Shaun becomes convinced that The Winchester, with its "big wooden doors," is the safest place to go. From the sozzled regulars to best friend Ed's (Nick Frost) reminders that "There's a Breville out back," this is a rather loving evocation of the pub as a consistent refuge from whatever London has to throw at you, even when the braindead army is climbing through its windows. In another example of London playing itself, the artsy Crouch End streets around The Winchester are shot in the traditionally working class area of New Cross.

The heavens open once again as I reach the site of The Duke of Albany, an impressive three-story Victorian building. Now, it's flats. Couldn't someone have at least erected a blue plaque? In my despair, I have forgotten that large swathes of the city have only been built in the time since the Blitz. In the 1949 Ealing Studios classic *Passport to Pimlico*, the residents of a Westminster district secede from Britain, largely because it means they will no longer have to abide by pub closing time. While much of the film was shot on the now rarely used studio lot, the north-of-river locations are all shot at real bomb-site exteriors on Lambeth Road, to the south. *Passport to Pimlico* may have had a sixth sense in predicting Brexiteer sentiment, and it's because of writer T. E. B. Clarke's understanding of the British relationship to the pub as intrinsically tied to historic fantasy. It's not quite the same levelling as the Blitz, but the fact that a large number of bars are no longer permitted licenses beyond midnight, or even 10 p.m. in Zone 1, has dramatically altered the London landscape. Turning swathes of the city into lifeless suburbs after the watershed speaks to authoritarian distrust of drinkers, as well as suspicion around the value of cultural spaces.

Cinematic institutions, in a reaction against accusations of pretension, have attempted to ape the communal style of the pub. Many cinemas, from Waterloo's BFI to Croydon's David Lean, attempt to appeal to accessible audiences using the techniques of the pub: quiz nights, DJ sets, and even Sunday lunches. These days you may be more likely to find APAs at a Murnau retrospective than at a pub.

This matches a larger change in consumption habits. Pubs have realised that higher turnovers are achievable through offering expensive food over housing a darts board. Around the same time, cinema venues have been regularly bought up and renovated by upscale chains including Picturehouse, Everyman, and Curzon, which have monopolised London's independent screens. To varying degrees, these chains offer the same thing: a boutique, upmarket version of the movie-going experience. They may need to split half the box office with distributors, but if you can justify charging theatre prices at the bar, the cinemas should be quids in – or so goes the theory.

So while Everyman et al. take over once glorious spots like Islington's Screen on the Green, which are content to shrink the programme while offering three small plate selections (served to your seat for £18.20), brands like Greene King gut classic drinking spots of their character, driving prices up without offering an experience of genuine quality. The most remarkable development of the gastro-revolution, in this writer's view, has been Wetherspoons' adoption of cinemas. The UK's pub chain giant, known for their cheap beverages and labyrinthine trips to the toilet, has taken up residence in a number of amazing old art deco cinemas, turning these former movie palaces into giant canteens. Two notable examples are The Capital in Forest Hill and Holloway Road's The Coronet, both of which have retained some features of their initial design while offering little room for a continuation of the history that both sites have as far back as vaudeville.

While any amount of sleaze occurs on Curry Club

Thursdays, there's not much of *Times Square Red, Times Square Blue* about these places. Something resembling an underground exists, however. Community cinemas and film clubs, being nimble and adaptable beasts, often take the form of pop-ups in the backroom of a pub. Many of these, including Double Wonderful and Tufnell Park Film Club, even create something close to a "vibe." The programmers at such events often attempt to form a direct relationship with their audience. A cinema where everybody knows your name. The Genesis Cinema, in Bethnal Green, has inverted this, by showing free screenings in its bar in a move that is, if not quite The Film-Makers' Cooperative, certainly the type of gimmick that Londoners are keen to post about. Cinemas are a place to escape your circumstances and to come alive; so, in fact, are pubs. If both are to survive, perhaps they need to unite entirely to make peace with their balance of public space and private establishment. What should a map be made of, if not the physical features of places that touch us, that draw us closer.

It's still raining on Monson Road as I leave The Duke of Albany. Later, I duck into the nearest local still standing – The Asylum – and try to articulate my findings about all this to the barman. He tells me he doesn't go to the cinema much. I think about asking him why, then I remember there's a print of *Dick Tracy* screening in an hour. I drink up. •

DRUNK LONDON

01 SALOON BAR

1940   dir. Walter Forde

In a cosy drinking den at Christmas, regulars try to prove their pal's innocence over one night at a London pub.

02 ALFIE

1966   dir. Lewis Gilbert

Michael Caine as a Cockney chauffeur ne'er do well – often seen womanizing, lying, or getting into pub brawls.

03 FRENZY

1972   dir. Alfred Hitchcock

Punters gossip in Covent Garden pubs over the identity of the "Necktie Strangler." Pity – barmaid Babs is next.

04 THE LONG GOOD FRIDAY

1980   dir. John Mackenzie

Bob Hoskins' Docklands developer gets entangled with the IRA – his pub, The Lion & Unicorn, gets blown up!

05 DANCE WITH A STRANGER

1985   dir. Mike Newell

Tells the story of Ruth, an unlucky-in-love barmaid; a climatic shooting takes place outside a Camberwell boozer.

06 WITHNAIL AND I

1987   dir. Bruce Robinson

Day drinking in Camden Town and Chelsea in this booze-soaked odyssey about two unemployed flatmates.

07 FACE

1997   dir. Antonia Bird

Lots of drinking and dying as Robert Carlyle is caught up in a botched heist in this pub-packed crime thriller.

08 LOCK, STOCK AND TWO SMOKING BARRELS

1998   dir. Guy Ritchie

East End geezer joint that made Guy Ritchie's name – a boozy ode to poorly-planned crime and crisp packets.

09 LEGEND

2015   dir. Brian Helgeland

Tom Hardy shines playing both Kray twins in a film of pub brawls, paranoid schizophrenia, and Philly mobsters.

10 MAN UP

2015   dir. Ben Palmer

London as whistlestop tour, about a drunken date that kicks off at Waterloo. Simon Pegg and Lake Bell star.

BLOWING UP
BLOW-UP

BY
MANUELA LAZIĆ

In a vision of '60s London replete with mods, mimes, and murder, a French Anglophile finds herself drawn to its ambiguous relationship with reality

"They don't mean anything when I make them," says the painter to his friend, the photographer, early on in Michelangelo Antonioni's *Blow-Up*. "Afterwards, I find something to hang on to." His works are abstract and made on instinct, but with time and distance, he's able to see shapes in them that almost seem human.

It's only now, almost 11 years after moving to London from my hometown in the middle of France, that I begin to make sense of the decisions that have led me here – not merely to England, but to film criticism, acting and filmmaking, and to writing this very piece. *Blow-Up*, a 1966 film set in London and directed by an Italian maestro, seems to have somehow played a major role in all of this.

The connection is in some respects obvious: Antonioni focuses on London when it was swinging and more glamorous than even his native Italy. In *Blow-Up*, coolness is dripping all over the place: from protagonist Thomas, played by a beady blue-eyed, Chelsea-boots-wearing David Hemmings, a beautiful fashion photographer who can make love to a woman through his camera; from his breezy studio and his stylish car that whizzes through the city freely; from the parties where well-dressed people share drugs and glances like there's no tomorrow and rock music is blasting through the cobwebs of British respectability; even Jane Birkin appears briefly, long before she became the epitome of French-British style by collaborating with Serge Gainsbourg, the coolest Frenchman who ever lived. So much swagger was bound to appeal to my teenage Anglophile taste buds.

I trace my passion for all things English to two teachers: Madame Gentil in secondary school, and Monsieur Guerlesquin in high school. The first was a true Brit, and as generous as her last name, which means "kind" in French, would suggest. She encouraged my sister and me to fan the flames of our burgeoning Anglophilia by joining a "European" track in high school, which meant that we'd get more classes taught in Shakespeare's language. This is where we found Monsieur Guerlesquin, a man always in a suit (despite it not being a requirement), who talked with a sophisticated RP and was determined to make us poor French speakers master the diphthong even if it meant losing all feeling in our faces. His dynamism and eccentricity made him a favourite of all students – even those who didn't love the language as much as I did. And if that weren't enough, he also happened to be a huge cinephile – probably the first one I ever met, I now realise – who I believe was aiming for a Hitchcockian effect with his outfit and typical stance, feet close to each other and arms held slightly back. He made us watch *The Dark Knight* without subtitles; deciphering what Christian Bale was saying in his cavernous bat-voice was perhaps his way of introducing us to the work required when listening to the many marvellous accents the UK has to offer, and which I would later encounter in London.

It was the opportunity to finally understand all the songs I loved that made me enjoy English so much – and yes, inevitably, discovering The Beatles was part of this journey. British music from the 1960s soon became my entire personality (which, at 16, maybe isn't saying much) and Tumblr blogs helped me discover other artists – T-Rex, David Bowie, and, one fateful day, Led Zeppelin. Jimmy Page, in particular, became my obscure object of desire, with his long black wavy hair, his flamboyant costumes, his devilish guitar playing. Perhaps it was on a fan blog that I first saw screenshots of his turn in *Blow-Up*, jamming alongside his former band The Yardbirds.

In the first few weeks of high school, my sister and I were spotted in a supermarket and encouraged to take part in a modelling contest, which led to us signing with an agency and devoting our school holidays (studies remained our priority) to castings in Paris and a few fashion weeks. In the French capital for perhaps a month, we somehow found out about the Forum des images, a cinema in Les Halles with repertory screenings every day and discounted prices for young people. The chain of events is now a blur, but we somehow managed to catch *Blow-Up*, which at this point we must have known took place in the world of fashion photography – a world we were just getting familiar with. What I remember for certain is our anticipation as we sat down to watch it.

I discovered much later just how consistently good Antonioni was at film endings – *L'Eclisse*'s is unforgettably simple and devastating – but the denouement of *Blow-Up* was a revelation. I didn't know, until then, that cinema could do such things. In the film, Thomas has been searching for material evidence of a murder he believes to have a photographic trace of, only to arrive at an impasse. The corpse has vanished and so have his pictures. Now, looking at mimes playing tennis with invisible rackets and balls, he has to accept that the connection between images and reality has been broken. As the mimes look at the imagined ball landing behind Thomas, Antonioni's camera follows it, first in the sky and then as it rolls on the ground. The director himself is creating an illusion of reality, a version of it without a centre, without a soul, much like the young people at The Yardbirds concert standing motionless, zombie-like. Thomas plays along and throws the ball back into the court. The camera stays on him and his eyes follow the ball as it bounces again between the two players. Soon, the sound of a real tennis match is heard – yet that match is out of frame. Antonioni pushes his argument even further, showing us how easily he can make us believe in an illusion with the power of his lens. I could not (and knew I should not) believe my eyes.

Throughout the film, Antonioni shows us that Thomas already has an inkling about this breakdown of meaning through his own work. "Even with beautiful girls, you look at them and that's that," he tells Jane (Vanessa Redgrave), the mysterious woman who won't let him keep the pictures he took of her and her lover in a park. As a fashion photographer, Thomas's job is to make the most out of that discrepancy between reality and images in order to create fantasy – but he seems to have stopped dreaming long ago. I think it was this critical take on the fashion industry that, paradoxically, also appealed to me at the time of my first viewing. I was myself sceptical of modelling and wasn't sure how to reconcile it with the idea I had of myself as a very studious and shy girl. As flattering as it was to be found beautiful enough for this trade, it felt threatening and, well, superficial. Seeing Antonioni express a similar ambiguity towards that world reassured me... yet looking back, I believe it must have also been exciting. The sense of risk perhaps felt like a challenge, even as it probably held me back.

It was only after I accepted that this work did not define my identity that I found some level of success with it – as *Blow-Up* demonstrated, my image was separate from who I was and I had no choice but to compartmentalise, which didn't feel natural, because it isn't. Thomas experiences this disconnect when he returns to the park to try and take a picture of the corpse he saw the night before. Finding nothing there, he crouches down, then looks up. Antonioni cuts from a shot on Thomas in that position to one on the branches blowing in the wind above him, before panning to reveal Thomas himself standing there. The effect is dissociative: Thomas seems to have jumped out of his own skin to look at himself. His own image is fractured and hard to pin down, as he realises that the world itself is gaslighting him and is not to be trusted. That cut, to me, still stands as one of the best in cinema history.

With every rewatch, my connection to *Blow-Up* deepens and I become better able to articulate what constitutes it. What struck me most this time was the typically British overcast day when Thomas ventures into the park for the first time (which he later describes as "beautiful" on account of it providing some great light for photographs), a detail that made me wonder about Antonioni's point of view on London itself as a foreigner. Was that white, cloudy sky as surprising to him, coming from sunny Italy, as it was to me, coming from a temperate climate in France? It seems that from his outsider's perspective, he could see that Swinging London was perhaps not much more than an idea, even as it was still supposedly unfolding. The hedonism of the mimes in the very first scene, as they drive around town screaming happily, always rings false to me, as though they are living a lie (and perhaps Antonioni's point in having them be mimes was precisely that they were).

The film's pessimism regarding the promises of the '60s is disquieting, as when Thomas forces young Birkin to strip naked and she proceeds to do the same to her girlfriend, but it is also perversely engrossing, giving London a darker undertone that appealed to me on my first viewing and still does today. As Thomas navigates the city in search of answers, we discover its hidden corners, which he perceives through new, or rather opened, eyes; the indifference of people towards each other or the truth strikes him at last, and I often felt similarly during my modelling years, working with designers who wouldn't acknowledge my existence even as I was trying on their clothes for them. It was the appearance of openness and coolness that mattered.

Watching Antonioni's other films, later on, I realised how perfect a subject Swinging London had been for him. In Italy, he had already made many masterpieces about the detachment and morbidity of modern life, focusing on deathly quiet new cityscapes and the impossibility of love in a world so cold. The burgeoning sexual revolution and the economic boom in '60s London made it a great place to further explore his theories about the consequences of the growing domination of industry and pretence; as much as I enjoyed *A Hard Day's Night* when I eventually watched it, I saw in it all of the things that Antonioni would dissect two years later in *Blow-Up*.

As my cinephilia developed and I eventually moved to London to do a Film Studies degree, I grew to appreciate Antonioni within the wider context of cinema history, as well as for his other films. His style, elliptical and precise, with almost Bressonian performances and a predilection for pregnant silences, remains endlessly intriguing to me as a writer and a filmmaker. *Blow-Up* inspires productive restraint and trust in the images and the spectator. At a time when many new films refuse to test their audience's patience with quietness and ambiguity, let alone challenge them on a deep, existential level, Antonioni's films are a reminder of what cinema can do, and how. The simplicity of the performances he captures encourages me to return to a more essential kind of acting in my own work, one that accepts the ambiguity of feelings and knows that this uncertainty – this fear mixed with desire – is what makes a performance ring true.

Blow-Up feels like a childhood memory now – my own Proust madeleine, taking me back to my Anglophilia, my early modelling days, and my passion for cinema, even as it continues to fascinate me. Looking at it up close, like Thomas searching for clues in his photograph, I can see in this film the myriad ways in which it influenced me. Ironically, this picture is not detached from my reality – it is part of it. •

LONDON IN THE SWINGING SIXTIES

01 A HARD DAY'S NIGHT

1964   dir. Richard Lester

36 hours of Beatlemania, in a film of surprising craft and vérité verve; the antithesis of "cash in."

02 THE PARTY'S OVER

1965   dir. Guy Hamilton

An American businessman's daughter falls in with a group of Chelsea Beatniks in this once controversial drama.

03 DARLING

1965   dir. John Schlesinger

Julie Christie plays a ballsy model who will stop at nothing to reach the top; like a gender-reversed *Alfie*.

04 MODESTY BLAISE

1966   dir. Joseph Losey

Pop art-inspired adapation of the comic book series is a campy delight – a kind of Mod take-down of Bond.

05 GEORGY GIRL

1966   dir. Silvio Narizzano

Swinging comedy with subtle dark notes, about a charming young woman (Lynn Redgrave) navigating adulthood.

06 BLOW-UP

1966   dir. Michelangelo Antonioni

A photographer accidentally captures a murder in a film that's as dangerous and flirty as a gust of wind up a mini-skirt.

07 BEDAZZLED

1967   dir. Stanley Donen

What if Faust, but in Sixties London? Stylish stuff from American Stanley Donen, with a proper lust for the era.

08 JOANNA

1968   dir. Michael Sarne

A bright, sexy tragi-comedy about a hedonistic art student in London, starring Geneviève Waïte.

09 PERFORMANCE

1970   dir. Nicolas Roeg, Donald Cammell

James Fox! Mick Jagger! Inspired casting in Cammell/Roeg's cool crime thriller, about a gangster taking refuge in Notting Hill.

10 DEEP END

1970   dir. Jerzy Skolimowski

Deeply weird tale of obsession. North London-set, but with a real feel for Soho's seedy underbelly.

PLEASE LOOK AFTER THIS BEAR

BY ELLA KEMP

Forget the marmalade sandwiches. The most British thing about Paddington? His origins as a refugee in London, grappling with cultural assimilation

One of my first experiences as a somewhat professional film critic was attending a screening of *Paddington 2* in 2017. I had missed the original film when it debuted to critical and commercial acclaim in 2014 and, having grown up in France, was unfamiliar with the classic books. Walking into Paul King's sequel that day, I had no expectations and no prior connection to Paddington's world.

Paddington 2 picks up where the first film left off, with the little brown bear, originally from Peru, now enjoying a new life in a postcard-worthy vision of London, alongside his found family the Browns. It didn't matter that I hadn't seen the original: *Paddington 2*, with its pantomime hijinks, gentle soul, and creative peaks, left a profound mark on me. Stepping out onto the street afterwards, I genuinely felt like something in my brain chemistry had been altered forever.

Over the years, both films have since become cherished comfort classics, offering me emotional support whenever the occasion calls for it. Yet it's only more recently that I've come to learn that Paddington's own story and history are so much closer to my own than I realised. It can be easy to brush off phenomena that win over the hearts of an entire nation, or across the world, as superfluous or basic or even trite (reducing British patriotism to a polite, naive talking bear can feel pretty laughable at the best of times). But what a wonder it is to realise that director Paul King's landmark films, based on author Michael Bond's iconic creation, have so much to say about where this great cinematic treasure sits in the wider landscape of our nation.

Bond was just twelve years old when he witnessed the Kindertransports bringing hundreds of refugee children, many of them Jewish, to Britain on the brink of World War II. They arrived by train at Reading station, and that image stayed with Bond his entire life. "They all had a label round their neck with their name and address on and a little case or package containing all their treasured possessions," the author told *The Guardian* in 2014 – before reflecting on his own creation, a little brown bear dressed in a navy blue duffle coat and a roomy red hat. "Please look after this bear. Thank you," reads a label around his neck.

"Paddington, in a sense, was a refugee, and I do think that there's no sadder sight than refugees," Bond said in that same interview. When considering what exactly constitutes a British film, or character, or symbol, Paddington Bear is one of the most weirdly emblematic things we have – after all, he shared his marmalade sandwich with the late Queen Elizabeth II over afternoon tea in 2022 to celebrate her Platinum Jubilee; almost 40 years prior, Bond had written the story *Paddington at the Palace*.

But look a little closer at Paddington's eyes and crucially his paperwork – or, actually, his lack thereof – and the most British thing about Paddington is, in fact, his legacy and poignancy as a Jewish refugee: like it or not, that's London in a nutshell, in all its multicultural and contradictory glory. A haven for those who come to the city in desperate need of a home they can finally call their own. My own family is Jewish, on both sides, though not in a hugely practising way on the day-to-day. But perhaps just as Paddington will keep a marmalade sandwich under his hat in case of emergencies, we will bake a honey and apple cake every September for Rosh Hashanah to welcome in a sweet and fruitful new year.

In 1938, rules forbidding Jewish refugees from entering the UK were relaxed after synagogues and Jewish-owned homes and businesses were destroyed across Germany and Austria. Jewish children (parents were not allowed to travel with them) came to the UK from Austria, Czechoslovakia, and Germany in the thousands from 1938 onwards in Kinderstransports – the first one arrived in Harwich on December 2, 1938, as 200 children fled a Jewish orphanage in Berlin, destroyed during Kristallnacht. Of some 10,000 children who travelled over, approximately 7,500, according to the United States Holocaust Memorial Museum, were Jewish.

Bond, who created Paddington in 1958 at the age of 32 – the year that his daughter Karen Jankel (today married to a Jewish accountant) was born – remembers those children. In the 2010 documentary *Paddington: The Man Behind the Bear*, Bond said of his own childhood: "We took in some Jewish children who often sat in front of the fire every evening, quietly crying because they had no idea what had happened to their parents, and neither did we at the time. It's the reason why Paddington arrived with the label around his neck."

The author also fondly looked back on what his own parents might have thought of the little bear themselves. "My mother wouldn't have been able to resist him; my father was a civil servant to the end of his fingertips, so he would have worried they weren't doing something official, but he would have helped," Bond told *The Telegraph*. "It was a kinder age." Although that might not fully sound like the London we live in today, it is the one we see in the *Paddington* films – one that gives hope that the fictional Brown family, with Sally Hawkins' kind eyes and Hugh Bonneville's bear-hug body language, could inspire some real-life Londoners, too.

Once Paddington arrives, the still-unnamed bear is met with kindness reminiscent of that shown by Bond's family, who find him at Paddington Station. In the first live-action film adaptation (coincidentally released the same year that the Immigration Act 2014 came into action in the UK, essentially allowing landlords to act as immigration officers and evict people without legal status), Mrs. Brown tells Paddington that he is a "very small bear" and asks where he's from. Paddington tells the kind lady that he is from "Darkest Peru" – Bond having gently been informed by his agent (more on him later) that there are no bears in "Darkest Africa" as he'd initially planned – before adding: "I'm not really supposed to be here at all. I'm a stowaway" (it's worth noting that any bears native to the UK were hunted out of existence hundreds of years ago). Mr. Brown initially shows hesitation in the books: in the second chapter of *A Bear Called Paddington*, he considers calling the authorities, confused and wary of what is essentially a wild animal. But his son Jonathan warns that the bear could get arrested, with Mrs. Brown noting: "It's not as if he's done anything wrong. I'm sure he didn't harm anyone travelling in a lifeboat like that."

When Bond was collaborating with filmmakers on the first live-action *Paddington* film in 2014, there was a suggestion that the Browns would instinctively take the bear to the immigration office – but that was deemed unacceptable. "Their first reaction is to take him off to the local immigration people, but I said: 'No way! There's no immigration at Paddington station.' I hate writing about things which don't exist," Bond said – a notion which the producers eventually came to agree with.

The parallels between Paddington's past and the real lives of thousands of immigrants entering the UK for decades are eye-opening, a testament to Britain and London specifically as a sometimes dangerous, sometimes life-changing and -saving new home for refugees like Paddington. Unfortunately, immigration lawyer Colin Yeo did in fact review the film for Free Movement and said: "I would assess Paddington's prospects of success before an immigration judge as virtually zero."

In 2009, Bond was among authors, actors (including Colin Firth, initially cast to voice Paddington before Ben Whishaw eventually took on the role – while the Ukrainian voice actor for the bear is, in fact, Jewish president Volodymyr Zelensky) and poets to sign a petition to then-Prime Minister Gordon Brown criticising the detention policy holding up to 2,000 children in centres by the UK Border Agency. It reads: "As writers and illustrators of books for children, we urge you to stop detaining children whose families have sought asylum in the UK. These children have already had their worlds torn apart and witnessed their parents in turmoil and in stress." The petition was sent with a note written "by" Paddington Bear. It reads: "Whenever I hear about children from foreign countries being put into detention centres, I think how lucky I am to be living at number 32 Windsor Gardens with such nice people as Mr. and Mrs. Brown. Mrs. Bird, who looks after the Browns, says if she had her way she would set the children free and lock up a few politicians in their place to see how they liked it!"

I can't imagine what that would feel like: as a Jewish child in the 1930s and 1940s, having to flee your home country, but also as a refugee coming from *anywhere* at any given moment. Writing this today just hammers home how lucky so many of us are, and how lucky I've been. Perhaps there is some subconscious salvation in the *Paddington* films to so delicately tell this young bear's story, while offering a comforting paw to all those watching who don't even realise his story could very well have been their own.

When in London, Paddington finds a kindred spirit with Samuel Gruber, a Hungarian antique dealer who owns Paddington's favourite shop on Portobello Road (which, in 1958 when the first Paddington book was written, saw the Afro-Caribbean community targeted for racial attack with ensuing riots lasting weeks – Bond and his first wife lived on Portobello Road in 1962). The character is based on a key figure in Bond's life, his first agent Harvey Unna – the man who did indeed know there were no bears in Africa. Bond was slightly less than pleased when Jim Broadbent was cast as Gruber in the films (who, for the record, gives a lovely performance) – for very specific reasons.

"It's not his fault, but it does bother me because I've such a clear picture of Dr. Gruber," Bond explained to *The Telegraph*. "I wanted someone foreign because he was based on my first agent [Harvey Unna], a lovely man, a German Jew, who was in line to be the youngest judge in Germany when he was warned his name was on a list. So he got out and came to England with just a suitcase and £25 to his name."

Gruber tells Paddington he, too, came to London following "trouble" in his home country, starting a new life for himself as a refugee. Unna was born to a middle-class Jewish family in Hamburg, forced to flee to Britain under the Nazis' anti-Jewish laws in 1933. In the films, Paddington and Gruber strike up a friendship over their shared love of beautiful things and the fight against some still intolerant parts of London (Peter Capaldi's spiky portrayal of Mr. Curry, the Browns' vitriolic, bigoted, yet undeniably farcical neighbor, perfectly encapsulates a more humorous take on the prejudice that characters like Paddington and Gruber originally faced).

Some of the most heartfelt moments in the films see Paddington struggling with cultural assimilation (how does a toothbrush work? Must you really always hold a dog on the Tube?) and we laugh, mainly because the films are ultimately kind-hearted and generous in their empathy of these situations. But what should make us feel proud and seen isn't quite the Browns' prim and proper Britishness – as Bond said to *The Telegraph* in 2008, "There is this side of Paddington the Browns don't really understand at all, what it's like to be a refugee, not to be in your own country."

That so many film lovers, myself included, may have rewatched these wonderful films countless times without understanding Paddington's history as an immigrant, or the parallels with Jewish refugees and the people his creator knew and loved, only reaffirms the integral part he plays in shaping how we view our city and our lives. To "other" him and those like him would be to turn against our own. The proudest thing we can do for our country is let them in. •

LONDON FOR THE FAMILY

01 PETER PAN

1953   dir. Clyde Geronimi, Wilfred Jackson, Hamilton Luske

Contains one of Disney's most magical sequences: a flight of fancy high over London that is pure euphoria.

02 101 DALMATIANS

1961   dir. Clyde Geronimi, Hamilton Luske, Wolfgang Reitherman

Regent's Park-set Disney caper; London is brought to life with bright colours and angular animation.

03 OLIVER TWIST

1974   dir. Hal Sutherland

Animated version of Charles Dickens' classic novel, notable for its vivid depiction of London's streets.

04 THE GREAT MOUSE DETECTIVE

1986   dir. Ron Clements, John Musker, Burny Mattinson, David Michener

Sherlock Holmes... with mice! Rousing adventure set in the city's gutters. The rain-swept climax on Big Ben is a highlight.

05 THE MUPPET CHRISTMAS CAROL

1992   dir. Brian Henson

Arguably the best Dickens adaptation ever, with Michael Caine playing it brilliantly straight as Scrooge. A hoot.

06 STEAMBOY

2004   dir. Katsuhiro Otomo

This steampunk adventure blasts through a fantastical vision of Victorian London, from the director of *Akira*.

07 FLUSHED AWAY

2006   dir. Sam Fell, David Bowers

A posh Kensington rat's sewer-bound adventure takes him to "Ratropolis," a version of London made from... trash.

08 THE PIRATES! IN AN ADVENTURE WITH SCIENTISTS!

2012   dir. Peter Lord

Stop-motion swashbuckling antics in this zany Aardman yarn, with roles for Queen Victoria and Charles Darwin.

09 MINIONS

2015   dir. Pierre Coffin, Kyle Balda

The Minions invade London, bringing their unique brand of mischief to Buckingham Palace and beyond.

10 MARY POPPINS RETURNS

2018   dir. Rob Marshall

Emily Blunt steps into Julie Andrews' shoes with aplomb; Lin-Manuel Miranda plays a cockney lamplighter (sorry).

IN THE CINE-TOURIST'S FOOTSTEPS

BY SAVINA PETKOVA

Mapping the city through cinema, one lecturer and film scholar's love of the streets bled into his life, and the lives of those he inspired...

hen I first moved to London in 2017, I made two friends: the cinema and the streets. Long before I even knew what psychogeography was – a concept I've since come to deeply appreciate, describing how our surroundings inform our personal connections – I was practising it just by way of living. For no more than a week, I could afford a quiet life: flat sitting for a friend in West London, volunteering at The Smalls Film Festival in East London, and a couple of £3 tickets at the BFI distracted me from the penniless, homeless, jobless present I had to deal with before the start of my master's degree. More often than not, I would walk all the way from East to West through City, Hyde Park, and Mayfair to save on the TfL fee and in the balmy days of August, not too dissimilar from the one where I sit now, writing this, I would chart my new life as a London-bound film person. Cinematically, it all seemed fitting.

I come from the outskirts of an Eastern European city ten times smaller, from a family that watches maybe one film per year, where my cinema education consisted not of repertory and arthouse hubs (they were too far downtown for me to be allowed to go), but a five-minute walk to a now-defunct multiplex. There, I dreamed of living in Italy not because I saw *Roman Holiday*, but because I watched Kristen Bell and Josh Duhamel fail at romance in *When in Rome*. Yes, I travelled outside of my hometown, I spoke fluent English, but I could never fake a native cinephilia.

Perhaps this is why for me, a London newcomer, experiencing places, sites, and streets had ambivalence baked into it. Recognising a filming location for me, the newborn cinephile, was a rarity to cherish. It soon became a running joke between me and my then-partner to comment on that corner of Brick Lane where Alicia Vikander's character in *Tomb Raider* makes a turn on her Deliveroo bike at the film's beginning. No matter the film, or the scene's origin, being bodily present in these spaces opens up something in the way one views the city: as a multi-layered, multi-purpose playground, an idea that very much goes against all that London is famous for (money, rats, skyscrapers, you name it).

I could always sense that architecture was cinematic material, without a doubt. But in addition to building its world from the ground up, it also serves as the connective tissue between places and people. To articulate this two-sided relationship, I turn to Giuliana Bruno – perhaps my biggest influence in writing about cinema – who writes of "geographies of emotion" and "emotion pictures." She highlights the role of affect in the way we relate to cinema, likening it to the corporeal way we are in the world. As we interact with places, their corners, cobblestones, and traffic lights, we are always mapping out new layers of personal experience on top of one another, often without noticing. By retreading the same path day after day, we leave a mark, dispensing with a tiny bit of the heel and sole with every step we take. In return, the ground absorbs our walking in a gesture of mutuality, albeit fleetingly. For everyone who has had the pleasure of walking through central London, rushing is the way to survive. That's why I think of these interactions with the city as inherently cinematic. In films,

Bruno writes, these relationships between people and place are transformed into "atlases of emotion," as per the title of her most famous book.

In February 2021, London – like the rest of the world – made for a troubling home. I'd been living in North London for less than a year when the pandemic hit. I had ended up there somewhat randomly, thanks to the kindness of two friends who were looking for a flatmate. But aside from the quirky name of Muswell Hill, I had no prior knowledge of this neighbourhood – residential, quiet, rich with exquisite pastry shops and fancy supermarkets. Yet it would only prove half a home. Quite frankly, being so far away from the BFI was becoming physically painful, even if it was still closed in lockdown. Unbeknownst to me, however, this particular corner of Haringey housed a slice of film history – one that would help me build a bridge between my personal past and present.

The first pedagogical figure in my life as a Film Studies student was Dr. Roland-François Lack, a kind and welcoming scholar who was something of an iconic figure in the UCL Humanities Department. Fitting for an institution which prides itself on interdisciplinarity, we Master's students were taught by cross-subject specialists, and Dr. Lack was one illustrious example. He had already been teaching at the university for more than 20 years, himself an alumnus of UCL, and his presence amplified the sense of belonging I felt to this strange new institution. These were my first weeks in UK education and the prospect of essay writing and workshops and seminars was as daunting as it was exciting. Early on, I understood Dr. Lack had written on a breadth of French subjects, names that meant a lot to me – Arthur Rimbaud, Robert Bresson – and names that meant little, like Jean-Luc Godard, or Éric Rohmer. I never told him I dislike Godard.

What struck me in those early days was the ease with which he spoke about early cinema's magic. I was in awe when I heard him explain how these pioneers constructed a visually graspable narrative through editing in motion. His passion for the past was vivid in the way he communicated with us students, always evoking references to his speciality, Francophone cinema and, in particular, the French New Wave. He was the one who showed us the (underseen, at least by film students!) 1965 anthology film *Six in Paris*. No wonder it later wound up serving as a blueprint for how I pictured Dr. Lack's relationship with cinema and the city. I was enchanted with the way he described Parisian streets and directors taking up their compact cameras to film a new kind of life – fictions of a city. I regret not speaking to him more and not recalling a particular conversation, as my shy self preferred to act like a sponge rather than a sounding board. Perhaps this sense of subdued grief is one of the reasons I am writing this essay in the first place.

When, in that dark February of 2021, I found out about Dr. Lack's untimely passing, the outpouring of sympathy in the academic and film criticism circles paid tribute to a special online archive of his: "The Cine-Tourist" (www.thecinetourist.net). In a short article for *Film Comment*, writer Violet Lucca described the website as "a brave new way of considering how filmmakers can fashion mise en scène from the world around them" and pointed out the idiosyncratic ways in which Dr. Lack brought together primary material, archival research, and site-specific context in his location breakdowns. Listing only places he himself had visited and gotten to know intimately, the website homepage reads:

> *The Cine-Tourist only writes about places that he knows, and since he doesn't travel much this site is chiefly about films made in Paris, Geneva and London (especially Muswell Hill, where he lives).*

Startled at the realisation we had briefly shared the same turf, I clicked through the parts of this archive I had until then neglected. The Cine-Tourist's shot and location analysis is so rich and detailed, unearthing every location from different angles and taking into account camera positions and actors' walking directions in many other parts of London, that I never even thought of zooming in on a random North London neighbourhood. Needless to say, the name "Muswell Hill" meant nothing to me before I ended up living there (since then, I've noticed how the mere mention of my dwelling place elevates me in the eyes of seasoned Londoners as I assimilate that extra clout).

It's a sad and perhaps banal fact that I came to appreciate my current London home only when a person, a symbol of my new life as a film person, had left it forever. But his spirit lives on. With the generous support of peers, colleagues, and friends, the Cine-Tourist website is preserved and, while no longer updated, remains an incredibly important source for studying filmic locations in British, French, and

Swiss cinema. This archive of knowledge and research also provides scholars and critics with the tools to decipher filmic places in a psychogeographic way (in short: an expression of the relationship between urban environments and individual emotions). Because Dr. Lack only wrote of places he knew well, he could peel the layers of history and show the past and present as co-existing through film screen grabs and Google Street View screenshots, often accompanied by photos he took himself. In the section named "How to map a film," one finds the following prompts which, when taken as a kind of recipe, open up new way of reading a film:

> how to film a map
> how to read a film, as a map
> how to read a film with a map (in your hand)
> how to read a map in a film
> how to read a map as a film

Charting a film's optical geometry through shot analysis (shot scale, camera angle, movement, framing) is an act of deep, meaningful engagement with its reality. What is often called the "pro-filmic" reality in a city-based film equates with real sites, even if the connection between them doesn't hold up to geographical validity. In a huge city like London, for example, shooting continuously with no topographical incongruencies is difficult and often unnecessary. In this way, the act of mapping a place through singular elements that come together to form a homogenous journey only in the edit is also an act of reverence to the magic of cinema. Dr. Lack knew this very well, and always pointed out the inconsistencies in a playful tone, giving probable explanations when possible. In this way, he provides a self-reflexive, personally-trodden atlas.

As per Bruno, "the atlas is not a map merely of spaces but of movements: a set of journeys within cultural movements, which includes movement within and through historical trajectories." History plays a role in the way the Cine-Tourist reconstructs places and their context, but his analysis is anything but purely historiographical. Whether he was thematically sketching the London from Aki Kaurismäki's 1989 film *I Hired a Contract Killer*, recounting the life of the Art Deco Odeon from 1936 (now the Everyman Muswell Hill), investigating building sites of interest, showcasing assorted stamps, or listing his favourite filmmakers, the Cine-Tourist never breezed through content, nor relied too much on systematising it. The website itself is an atlas-collage, a horizontal structure with a sidebar menu that places Agnès Varda, maps in books, Robert W. Paul and Walter R. Booth (resident Muswell Hill filmmakers) side by side in a rich tapestry of interconnected cine-meanings. Dr. Lack's ability to trace intertextual links and braid beautiful threads out of them was evident not only in his teaching, but in the anti-canonical way he constructed his online archive.

One of my favorite parts of the website showcases screen grabs from inconspicuous scenes – barely noticeable backgrounds in 90s dramas and comedies – that Dr. Lack's keen eye has identified as Muswell Hill locations. We have Crocodile Antiques at 120 Muswell Hill Broadway in Mike Leigh's *Secrets and Lies*, nested in between other small shops in a tracking shot. Or snippets of the glorious Alexandra Palace (where, we learn in another section of the website, a film studio existed for merely three years) in Anthony Minghella's *Breaking and Entering*, Clint Eastwood's *Hereafter*, and Stefan Schwartz's *Shooting Fish*. Ephemeral locations exist alongside one another with complex cartographies: they can go on for paragraphs and rely on multiple shots to piece the location together. There is no hierarchy, just an ever-present love of film spaces.

In all his curiosity and impressive knowledge, the Cine-Tourist is never dogmatic. His vocabulary makes room for doubt, with his "I think"-s, or "It looks like" interjections. Occasionally, he's unable to identify a spot, and he admits it with a dignity few academic writings would afford. These gaps are somehow necessary, especially in a place like London, whose features are destined never to remain the same. They signify that a city can be yours, even if it is ultimately unknowable. •

This essay is dedicated to the memory of Dr. Roland-François Lack (1960-2021)

VISITING LONDON

01 PASSPORT TO SHAME

1958   dir. Alvin Rakoff

A French maid is lured to London under false pretenses and forced into sex work – Diana Dors helps her escape.

02 HUSBANDS

1970   dir. John Cassevetes

Gazzara, Falk, Cassavetes: all the boys! They're married men who hightail it to London during a boozy midlife crisis.

03 A WARM DECEMBER

1973   dir. Sidney Poitier

Poitier finds love with a mysterious woman while on a month-long trip to London. Dripping with cool '70s 'fits.

04 BRANNIGAN

1975   dir. Douglas Hickox

John Wayne in London: as weird as seeing a white rhino. He's a Chicago cop sent to London to extradite a mob boss.

05 THE GREAT MUPPET CAPER

1981   dir. Jim Henson

Kermit, Fozzie & co. are sent to London to investigate a stolen necklace – a stealth Busby Berkeley musical.

06 A FISH CALLED WANDA

1988   dir. Charles Crichton

Jamie Lee Curtis plays a hilarious criminal who's drafted to London as part of an elaborate jewel heist.

07 THE PARENT TRAP

1998   dir. Nancy Meyers

Lindsay Lohan genuinely robbed of awards for her dual turn in this twin-swap caper, set in London and the US.

08 KABHI KHUSHI KABHIE GHAM...

2001   dir. Karan Johar

An Indian man, desperate to reunite his family, travels from Delhi to London. Bollywood musical sequences galore.

09 LAST CHANCE HARVEY

2008   dir. Joel Hopkins

Cutesy romance about a jingle writer (Dustin Hoffman) who falls for an airport worker at Heathrow (Emma Thompson).

10 YARDIE

2018   dir. Idris Elba

Idris Elba went behind the camera for this 80s tale, about a Jamaican gangster seeking revenge in Hackney.

FAKE IT WHILE YOU MAKE IT

BY ADAM SOLOMONS

Capturing the capital has never been a straightforward affair. Some of the city's best cinematic depictions are mere illusions – though these warped portraits often locate a finer truth

The story of the most famous photo of London ever taken is also a handy illustration of the city's identity in cinema: imperious, yes, and a little dishonest. In the middle of a night-time German bombing raid in late December 1940, photographer Herbert Mason went up to the roof of the *Daily Mail* office and saw St Paul's Cathedral lit up by the fires of ruined buildings around it. Emerging from a blanket of grey smoke coating the City, the dome of Christopher Wren's masterpiece stood tall out of the surrounding wreckage. The picture was swiftly signed off by the censors and splashed on the *Mail*'s front page the following day: "War's Greatest Picture," the headline read, "St Paul's stands unharmed in the midst of the burning city." Unsurprisingly, the picture was also used by the Germans to illustrate how well the Blitz was going.

St Paul's would remain untouched in the final five months of the bombing, and Mason's picture would be immortalised as a portrait of London's enduring spirit. Two months prior, *The Great Dictator* had been released, with Charlie Chaplin making his climactic impassioned speech about how "the Kingdom of God is within all man" in front of a painted backdrop of St Paul's. No matter that Mason's image had been heavily edited, the burning and broken buildings around it cropped out, the Cathedral itself guarded by a special unit of firefighters ordered by Churchill to protect the "symbol of fortitude" before it had even become one.

Tales told about London have always been better than

the truth: London Bridge never did fall down, and you *are* more than six feet away from a rat.

As the city's identity was slowly shaped by tabloid legend and ascientific claims about its rodent population, cinema's production designers and art directors looked to have taken note. Their stylised versions of London, a fixture of British cinema since its birth, have done much more to shape cinemagoers' understanding of London than exterior shots of the city in the cold light of day. In fact, these film artists' illustrations forged my own conception. A few weeks before my third birthday, my family left our shop front-turned-home in Hackney to settle in Essex, a county of exiled Cockneys. My understanding of my birthplace was as hazy and unreliable as the films set in London seemed to show. But what they also did, and still do, was depict a city as the centre of the modern universe with a gravitational pull to match. That's to say that the London of film is one for nostalgic quasi-outsiders, not those lucky (unlucky?) enough to know the real thing.

There are a few reasons why filmmakers depicting London so often opt for style over substance. Compared to New York, London's natural cinematic qualities leave much to be desired. Our capital is less dramatic (or tall), its people famously introverted, and most of its older streets too narrow, labyrinthine, and hilly for straightforward filming. Another reason is London's sheer scale: by 1911, the city's population had ballooned to more than seven million, making it the biggest city in the world and the biggest city there had ever been. Nuance is the enemy of a simple story; a modest stage can hold a much more convenient setting than the awkward, ever-changing metropolis itself. All this has made London more established as a complicated, moveable setting rather than a character in the films set there, and is part of why "London movies" are less of a thing than "New York movies," "Paris movies," "Rome movies," and so on. It's no surprise that London housed 30 film studios by 1910, many of which were dedicated to carefully recreating the city in which they found themselves. It was the set dressers and production designers on these lots who helped filmmakers invent an identity for London onscreen.

The Great Dictator was far from the first film to show a stylised London to make a point, political or otherwise. Henry Edwards' 1916 film *East Is East* showed squalor in a wonky Poplar tenement and the high life of a Home Counties manor via a spacious sound stage at Hepworth Studios in Walton-on-Thames, Surrey, where early adaptations of *Alice in Wonderland* from 1903, *David Copperfield* from 1913, and *The Hound of the Baskervilles* from 1921 were also made (in case you thought the glut of IP was a new thing). Some '20s pictures did shoot on location: take 1922's *Sam's Boy*, about an orphan forced to sleep rough on London's docklands; E.A. Dupont's transgressive 1929 drama *Piccadilly*, shot at numerous iconic London locations; Anthony Asquith's stylish early noir *Underground*, which notably used the active Lots Road Power Station as an eerie real-life backdrop; and Alfred Hitchcock's 1929 film *Blackmail*, which features chases on the Kingsway in Westminster and outside the British Museum. The vast majority of the era's films, however, were shot at studios in Twickenham, Islington,

Denham, Teddington, Elstree, or Ealing, where Alfred Hitchcock had incidentally worked as a set dresser. Although the *New York Times* celebrated *Piccadilly*'s "verisimilitude," the new expenses associated with sound made the cheapness of shooting pomp and Poplar in the same place a virtual necessity. At least at the beginning, London's stylised cinema identity was forged out of obligation. The forgery was beautiful.

Having modernised its stages in 1931, Ealing Studios would soon become the ultimate location for the new fictional London to be built, painted, and broadcast to the world. That it was a "postage stamp" in size compared to the capital's other studios, according to one visiting journalist, would become an asset. A generation's pre-eminent production designers would walk through its doors and, usually, stay there, with staff, stars, and filmmakers kept on contracts against industry convention.

The studio's golden era began with the arrival of producer Michael Balcon in 1938, where he championed a genre that would solidify the capital's film identity and change British cinema forever: the Ealing Comedy. 1941's *Passport to Pimlico* playfully speculated about the consequences of a forgotten central borough declaring its independence. Perhaps unwittingly, that film's greatest contribution to the depiction of London on film is in its portrayal of the pub as the social and intellectual hub of the new republic, where all news is broken, sorrows drowned, and highs celebrated. Reportedly this was modelled on The Red Lion, across the street from Ealing Studios, where the cast and crew would let off steam after a day's work.

In his invaluable book *The Secret Life of Ealing Studios*, Robert Sellers writes that Ealing films had a natural community feel that stemmed in large part from the working arrangements of those stationed there. Martin Scorsese in a foreword to the book writes that Ealing comedies were genuinely "hand-made," a useful term that applies both to their productions and, by extension, London's look in the movies of the day.

But Ealing wasn't just a community studio in how it was run. Its films helped popularise a version of a city that, despite its size, was inherently quaint. Admittedly London's exteriors did occasionally make that job easier: Mrs. Wilberforce's fake cul-de-sac house in 1955's *The Ladykillers* could be a miniature from *Thomas the Tank Engine*. She defeats Alec Guinness's gang of quirky criminals with virtue, while the residents of Pimlico do indeed agree that a good time at the pub was all they were really after, anyway. Black comedies they were, but with a wholesome edge and a simple idea about the way people are that could be captured by a few artists, with a few brushes, in a handful of rooms.

Decades of fake London onscreen culminated in the 1968 adaptation *Oliver!*, shot on sprawling, outwardly synthetic sets that bear little resemblance to The Big Smoke – or the social realism of Charles Dickens' novel. Filmed on six sound stages and the ten-acre backlot at Shepperton Studios, Carol Reed's Best Picture-winning musical is a schmaltzy adaptation of Lionel Bart's schmaltzy musical that sought to recast Oliver Twist's aimless and arduous journey through early-Victorian London as an adventure toward health and happiness. Sixties Britain ate it up like a hearty pot of gruel.

Aesthetics and ideas found a perfect match in Reed's direction, which deferred to the colourful fantasies of the musical version in its conception of two Londons: Nancy's pub and Fagin's den versus a civilised society and the leafy square by Mr. Brownlow's house. Respectability and sordidness smashed together, the sheer denseness of London making such a contrast work on a single theatre stage. Reed's film feels similarly artificial. And, somewhere in the distance as Nancy ambles among the sewage between the pub and the den, St Paul's.

Boy chimney sweeps emerge steaming from the top of posh houses in *Oliver!*, dusting themselves off in time to "Consider Yourself," while Fagin's child goons sing about their eyes popping out when they get hanged in "I'd Do Anything" (that's the closest we get to an actual hanging in *Oliver!*, unlike the book). *Oliver!* is, of course, a musical, but its flippant attitude toward those at the receiving end of Victorian-era injustice places it among similarly rosy-eyed visions of London, like David Lean's questionable telling of the same story from 20 years beforehand. Nonetheless, the cor, blimey! Londons of *Oliver!*, *My Fair Lady*, and *Mary Poppins* (the latter two, both 1964) profited from a counter-revolutionary nostalgia as the Swinging Sixties raged on.

The return of outdoor London as the predominant face of the city in movies came gradually, and it marked a significant shift in filmmaking priorities. This change was, much like the rise of fake London, largely cost-driven, as shooting on location could often prove more economical than constructing elaborate sets. The advent of new technology, particularly the development of more sophisticated microphones, made it easier to capture clear sound during exterior shoots, enabling filmmakers to embrace the dynamic and unpredictable energy of real cityscapes. At the same time, a cultural shift within British cinema played a critical role: the growing popularity of realist filmmaking among influential, avant-garde directors. This movement, inspired by a desire to connect audiences with authentic, relatable narratives, elevated The Real World to a new level of prominence. As a result, carefully styled backdrops were abandoned, with production designers ceding control over the meticulously crafted universes of their films in favor of the spontaneity and authenticity of real-world settings, allowing London itself to become an integral character in these stories. This evolution not only transformed how films portrayed the city but also reflected broader societal trends toward realism and a fascination with urban life as it was truly lived.

But it would be a stretch to argue that the city's films have lost out per se: Mike Leigh's more authentic London films have helped redefine the cinematic identity of the city we love, the gritty hard edges fostering a singular beauty of their own. Unlike the polished, imagined versions of fake London built on sound stages or recreated abroad, Leigh's London feels lived-in and real. His work shows that the city doesn't need gloss or artifice to stand out. By embracing the raw details of the real city, his films prove that authenticity can be just as captivating as any carefully constructed fantasy.

It's also untrue that fantasy London has disappeared from sound stages altogether, with Yorgos Lanthimos' steampunk Victorian London in 2023's *Poor Things* as distinct as any recent film setting. The Golden Lion winner's dreamlike metropolis was created on 14 acres of sound stages and backlots in Budapest. And like the great Londons of cinema's olden days, it makes no effort to be realistic. In fact, the joy is in its surrealism, brown cardboard-looking rooftops that stretch out forever, a fortress-like Tower Bridge even grander than the real thing. Yet although a terrific, highly acclaimed film, the aesthetics (never mind the economics) of *Poor Things* feels decidedly vintage, an irreverent mockery of a silly city and its even sillier people. That seems to be the point. It's an appropriately childish view of London that, I was elated to see, gets pretty close to my own. •

HEIGHTENED LONDON

01 MARY POPPINS

1964   dir. Robert Stevenson

A fake London of chimney tops and catchy tunes – for many, the definitive vision of the city on screen.

02 OLIVER!

1968   dir. Carol Reed

Studio-bound Dickens adaptation plays like a tourist fantasy-cum-theme park. Behold, LondonWorld!

03 BEDKNOBS AND BROOMSTICKS

1971   dir. Robert Stevenson

Portobello Road is immortalised as an all-singing, all-dancing cultural melting pot where you can buy anything.

04 HARRY POTTER AND THE PHILOSOPHER'S STONE

2001   dir. Chris Columbus

London as cosy nostalgia machine, with early portions set amidst cobbled streets and one iconic station.

05 SWEENEY TODD: THE DEMON BARBER OF FLEET STREET

2007   dir. Tim Burton

Victorian squalor captured with gusto by Burton, just before he succumbed to a tragic CGI addiction.

06 SHERLOCK HOLMES

2009   dir. Guy Ritchie

All of Richie's output is heightened London, in a way – this, a steampunk vision fashioned as a romp.

07 THE IMAGINARIUM OF DOCTOR PARNASSUS

2009   dir. Terry Gilliam

Underrated Gilliam offering set in a scuzzy Victorian London (his *Brazil* was also London in all but name).

08 KINGSMAN: THE SECRET SERVICE

2014   dir. Matthew Vaughn

This increasingly inane franchise started strong, with early action spread across council estates and pubs.

09 PADDINGTON

2014   dir. Paul King

London's trademark grit is sanded off to pave the way for King's joyous, utopian rendering of the city.

10 POOR THINGS

2023   dir. Yorgos Lanthimos

The city gets an eerie, steampunk overhaul in this creatively filmed take on the "unfilmable" novel.

THE LAST PICTURE SHOW

BY STEPH GREEN

In a forgotten patch of North London suburbia, a rich cinematic history has fallen prey to vinegar syndrome. A century later, a community is fighting to restore its reputation

I n September 1940, 14-year-old Phyllis Yorke was an ordinary teenage girl in extraordinary circumstances. The Battle of Britain had begun in earnest, with a Luftwaffe parachute mine having already blown the glass clean out of her house's window panes – twice. At school, when not cowering in a shelter with her friends, she would nibble on a sandwich – Marmite and raw carrot, or occasionally baked beans – and wait for the wailing siren to end. But among the sounds of doodlebugs, the inky blackouts, and meagre rations... a kaleidoscopic light at the end of the tunnel. The escapist possibilities of the Palmadium Cinema, where she remembers sneaking away to watch *Snow White and the Seven Dwarfs.*

Christine Collins' mother used to go to the Palmadium twice a week when she was a teenager in the 1930s, just as Britain was experiencing its own Great Depression. While glued to the screen – she went twice a week because that is how often they changed the programme – she would feast on a cream tea. Fresh brews, scones, clotted cream, and jam were set on small tables, gently lit by dim lamps, on the raised section that ran along the left-hand side of the auditorium. Her mother couldn't remember what she enjoyed more: the films, or the cream tea.

Take a look at the many blog posts, Facebook groups, and online community dashboards dedicated to Palmers Green's past, and you'll find countless memories of the Palmadium, which opened one frosty Christmas Eve in 1920 to grand pomp and ceremony. A front-page advertisement in the *Palmers Green & Southgate Gazette* promised that it would "present the finest pictures" with a "stupendous programme," noting that the dazzling opening gala would feature a screening of the five-reel 1919 picture *The Virtuous Model*, starring Dolores Cassinelli. A West End Orchestra made the pilgrimage up to this Enfield suburb to perform on opening night, as newspapers would enthusiastically declare it "London's first Super Cinema."

Seating a staggering 2,188 audience members, the Palmadium boasted not one but two circles, a large orchestra pit, an organ, and fourteen boxes. It was designed in the Beaux-Arts style: resplendent with red brickwork and sage-green tiles in Palmers Green's high street. "Much praise is due to the architect," writes a 1921 article in the now-defunct *Kinematograph Weekly*, "for having designed a kinema containing so many beauties of architecture [...] the interior is built on the canti-lever system – thus ensuring a perfect view of the screen from every seat in the house." It was even a place that encouraged film criticism and cinephilia: "Each week there is an essay competition with a prize of £5. Competitors have to give their opinions on the acting and general production, and why they like or dislike the film. This is a great hit with the patrons."

At a 1926 parliamentary hustings, Lord Walter Phillimore, a British lawyer and judge, said:

> *"I think [it] is one of the finest halls in London, though it is not generally known. It is called the Palmadium, and is in the North of London. I had never heard of the district, and I am ashamed to say I have forgotten it. I said to someone who knew that part of London:*

"What is that district, and what sort of people am I going to speak to? "He said: "It is a dormitory." The City of London at this moment is ringed round with dormitories, that is to say, with places to which the true citizens of London, who do their work in London, who earn the wealth of London, who make the character of London [...] Those are the true citizens of London, for whom you should have churches built."

Lord Phillimore was participating in a Hansard debate about the preservation or demolition of churches. But he raised an interesting point on the population of this place: who they were, what they deserved, and why.

I walked down Green Lanes recently to try and find a trace of the long-gone Palmadium Cinema (which was renamed the Gaumont in 1951 before being demolished in 1961, bowing out with a showing of the Dirk Bogarde western *The Singer Not the Song*). Green Lanes is one of London's longest roads, linking the northernmost borough of Enfield, through Palmers Green, and all the way down to trendy Stoke Newington; visit on a Saturday night and its Turkish restaurants spill out onto the street like an overstuffed dolma. Passing a travel agent with ancient computers, several cafés guarded by moody blokes in puffer jackets smoking cigarettes, and a man spitting on the pavement outside NatWest, I walked trepidatiously up to the site of the old picturehouse. Horror: the space is now occupied by a branch of MERKUR Slots. I look down at the picture of the old building on my phone, then up again at the grey, perpendicular architecture standing in its place. At that moment, it felt like cinema had never been so far away.

MERKUR Slots is a 24-hour casino that emerged after an unsuccessful campaign was launched in 2021 to prevent yet another gambling establishment from opening on the high street; at the time of writing, another petition is circulating to prevent a sixth betting shop from opening. On the community website *Palmers Green Jewel in the North*, which explores the history of this suburb, the admin writes: "Can you imagine what it would be like to be for Palmers Green to have a department store, two cinemas, and no betting shops or nail bars?" But residents aren't just complaining about the betting shops. There's another petition circulating, too: pleading for public support to open a cinema, to fill one of the several vacant retail spaces on the high street. They're not asking for the Palmadium: just somewhere, somehow, to watch a film.

As a film critic, cinephile, cinema-lover, and local resident, I've been relatively ignorant of Palmers Green as a cultural crater, content to travel into central London if I want to catch a specific repertory film, or hop on the bus to my nearest multiplex, Vue Wood Green (a rather cursed and liminal space, but steadfastly committed to charging only £6 if you're happy to sit through something with a name like *Madagascar 3: Europe's Most Wanted*). At £17 a pop, the Everyman cinemas in Barnet and Muswell Hill are inaccessible at best, and can feel like daylight robbery at worst. Cinema in this pocket of North London doesn't feel readily accessible, or even important at all. The community petition suddenly – like a footie agnostic watching England in a World Cup penalty shoot-out – made me surge with galvanizing pride. I signed and shared it immediately.

One of my earliest memories involves cinema and Palmers Green. It is April 2003 and I am five years old, holding my mum's hand as the sun begins to set on Green Lanes. Wearing a light blue puffer coat and standing with a large crowd, I watch as a camera crew bustle around a triple-decker purple bus; unbeknownst to me, they are filming the Knight Bus sequence for *Harry Potter and the Prisoner of Azkaban*. Even then, I recall how tangible and exciting this cultural proximity felt: the cameras, the clapperboards, the cordons. The glamour of art within my quotidian surroundings. A community that had turned out, teeth chattering, to catch a glimpse of cinema in the making.

So perhaps it wasn't surprising that this same community had signed – with three thousand residents pledging their signatures in less than a week – a petition calling for their own cinematic space. "Palmers Green is a diverse community. It's a *mezze* of different people," Sam Neophytou, owner of ArtHouse cinema in Crouch End, tells me. He's spent four years trying to expand operations to Palmers Green and open a cinema here. The issue? The community, according to the petition, is "being held to ransom by indifferent landlords who prefer to leave their large units empty."

For Sam, community effort is important, but not enough: "Until there is action from above, which means the council taking some control over the high street, then you're not going to get these things. It's basically a case of convincing landlords that you're actually doing something worthwhile, which is going to regenerate the high street, which is going to regenerate their property and bring life to the whole community. But I'm afraid you don't get landlords particularly interested in that."

It hadn't occurred to me that there was actually financial backing and popular interest in opening a cinema, and that the problem lay at the feet of greedy landlords who seem content to turn Palmers Green into a sub-par Atlantic City that smells vaguely like souvlaki (not that there's anything wrong with that last part). I had unknowingly, for years, been ignorantly reaping the benefits of volunteer-led initiatives; genuine community effort done for no pay. The pop-up tap room. The new artwork on the railway bridge. The Stevie Smith poetry plaque – *"The pleasures of friendship are exquisite,/ How pleasant to go to a friend on a visit!"* – memorialising the past literary resident by the station. The cleaner pavements. The non-profit community interest shop, Philanthropy, that employs adults living with mental health issues or who have learning disabilities, from which I've decorated my flat and decked out my wardrobe. Talkies is another volunteer-led, not-for-profit organisation seeking to make film-going accessible in the local area as a sticking plaster for the lack of nearby picturehouse; the group regularly programmes events at venues across Palmers Green, and neighbouring Enfield and Winchmore Hill. "We are unashamedly suburban," says founder David Williamson. "We are definitely not Hackney, or Shoreditch, or the West End, or Southbank. Nor are we trying to be."

These initiatives don't feel like gentrification: rather, a genuine investment into a seemingly forgotten suburb, a "dormitory" with history to tell, and communities desperate to save it from being yet another high street dying a slow death to vape shops.

I began thinking about that word, community, and cinema as community. Not necessarily an experience that needs to be shared, per se – for so many people, it's still a space to hide in the dark, often on their own, and escape into a story – but as the very *opposite* of a liminal space, an empty building, a transitory area. A space with purpose, discernible and palpable, that demands stillness and consideration. These are the spaces that are fast falling off our collective cultural maps, particularly in non-inner-city locales.

It would be insensitive, and a stretch, to waffle about "the power of cinema" when people in London (and indeed around the country) are struggling to heat their homes or feed their families, but movies have long acted as a salve that binds a community together in harsh times. Charlie Chaplin's comedies were catnip to those trudging through the effects of the Great Depression during the 1930s, while in the midst of World War II, Hollywood made it their duty to entertain, motivate, and lift the spirits of the people. These were the golden years of cinema-going, peaking in 1946 with 1.6 billion recorded admissions in the UK (by way of comparison, 2019 saw 176 million attendees: just 11% of this heyday). Despite the shift towards streaming, film remains an important binding tool; during the COVID-19 pandemic, over 10 million users made use of the Teleparty plug-in to watch films at the same time as their friends while siloed away, typing inane things in the right-hand chat column to let the others know they were still there, watching along with them.

This is reflected back at us within film, given that directors have long been enamoured with reflecting the experience of cinemagoing on-screen. Whether it's Mia Farrow using moviegoing as an EpiPen for her dull life in *The Purple Rose of Cairo* or cinema's microcosmic pleasures in Tsai Ming-liang's *Goodbye, Dragon Inn*, depictions of community cinemagoing are rife on the silver screen, each one quietly affirming its importance within our lives. Take Peter Bogdanovich's *The Last Picture Show*, in which two friends living in a tiny, declining town reconcile at the final showing at the sole cinema in the area, which is imminently drawing the curtain. "Won't be much to do in town with the picture show closed," laments Jeff Bridges' character, Duane. The closure of the picturehouse reflects the death of youthful possibility itself.

Or the scene in Preston Sturges' *Sullivan's Travels*, in which prisoners in a work camp are allowed a rare reprieve in the form of a film showing. Filing solemnly into a nearby church, setting their weary bodies down among the pews, the men sit and watch as the projector unspools Walt Disney's 1934 cartoon *Playful Pluto*. Joel McCrea, playing John L. Sullivan, finds himself laughing along despite his misery, spurred by the raucous merriment of his fellow men. Case in point: one of the most beautiful sequences put to film, in Terence Davies' *The Long Day Closes*, when a camera floats over a cinema audience, surveying them in an elegiac God's view pan, before tracking continuously over a church congregation lined up in neat pews.

In Marielle Heller's *Can You Ever Forgive Me?*, Richard E. Grant's Jack Hock tries to remember an old acquaintance: "She died… Or maybe she didn't die. Maybe she just moved to the suburbs – I always confuse those two." The suburbs have long been the butt of the joke, depicted as an artless purgatory between the countryside that inspires and the city that energises. But Palmers Green, seemingly as discreet and dismissible as it was a hundred years ago, deserves more than a fading parade of betting shops. "We need to start looking at the beauty of these diverse suburbs," says Sam. "If we have a resource here to bring those communities together, just see how wonderful that could be." A pause. "I think that's what's sad. That politicians, and the council, and people in those kinds of places, don't resource the arts in that sense. The arts are the only thing that really changes the face of humanity. That's what cinemas do. That's what they enable, by putting on wonderful films that actually serve their communities."

Over a century ago, at the Palmadium, the manager's aim was "to provide for the district what it has wanted for a long time – a well-appointed theatre presenting the best pictures." Nothing has changed. It can happen again.

Lord Phillimore's words echo in my ear: *"Those are the true citizens of London. For whom you should have churches built."* •

NORTH LONDON

01 SAPPHIRE

1959   dir. Basil Dearden

Hampstead Heath whodunnit, as an open-minded detective trawls through clues and uncovers racial tension.

02 BUNNY LAKE IS MISSING

1965   dir. Otto Preminger

Or did she ever even exist? A mother desperately searches Hampstead for a trace of her vanished daughter.

03 A LIZARD IN A WOMAN'S SKIN

1971   dir. Lucio Fulci

Giallo film titles go hard – and this one's no exception. Look out for an extended set piece at Alexandra Palace.

04 HELLRAISER

1987   dir. Clive Barker

Suburbia is hell – literally – on a residential street in Cricklewood, as demons raise Cain on Dollis Hill Lane.

05 RIFF-RAFF

1991   dir. Ken Loach

Ex-con Robert Carlyle takes a job on a Tottenham building site in this indictment of poor working conditions.

06 CAPTIVES

1994   dir. Angela Pope

Tim Roth is a sexy felon who woos an uptight dentist. Set in/around Southgate, this is a rare, fiery British erotic thriller.

07 THIS YEAR'S LOVE

1999   dir. David Kane

Kathy Burke is the standout in this tale of six Londoners navigating love and heartbreak in buzzing Camden.

08 THE LOW DOWN

2000   dir. Jamie Thraves

Turn-of-the-millennium ennui in Hackney, as Aidan Gillen (with great hair) mulls over his erratic love life.

09 DREAMS OF A LIFE

2011   dir. Carol Morley

Haunting docu-drama set in a Wood Green flat, where life and death seem to go unnoticed.

10 SURGE

2020   dir. Aneil Karia

Ben Whishaw goes on a crime spree across the capital, predominantly set in Tottenham and Finsbury Park.

CRONENBERG'S LONDON

BY RORY DOHERTY

In the 21st century, the Canadian auteur shifted to London for a pair of gruelling features. The ever-changing capital proved a perfect fit for his audacious sensibilities set myself a challenge: I will walk from the Prince Charles Cinema back to my girlfriend's flat from memory. I've been visiting London every other month for about two years, hoping the perks of free accommodation in the city centre will make up for the pain of loving someone long-distance, and have yet to walk anywhere without staring at Citymapper on my phone every step of the way.

I live in Edinburgh, a village compared to London, where the street corners and building facades are imprinted on my brain. They appear in my mind's eye whenever I talk, whenever I think, whenever I write. The city is quietly marked across the inside of my body like hidden tattoos that can only be enjoyed by the mortician who opens me up on the slab. When I wander London, I feel like I'm looking at photos of it.

To the millions of people living within London's sprawling boundaries, it is a city undergoing unceasing change. It's a cliché that London is less of a unified state and more of an overstuffed collection of villages, with each of its parts subject to regeneration and neglect that may be outside its control and do not contribute to city-wide unity. Outsiders can clearly spot London's decoherence; the city doesn't seem to change with clear, organised, municipal logic, but more like a system of unwavering, precoded survival instincts. It's less municipal and more biological, predictable patterns that never make it clear if there will be a completed, finished product. And if anyone is going to view a city as a mutating, germinating living thing, it's David Cronenberg.

Cronenberg's two films set in the capital – 2002's *Spider* and 2007's *Eastern Promises* – characterise London as a space that ushers in the kind of change that its population is powerless to influence or obstruct. At the same time, the city absorbs the traumas and identities of the people that live there, ingesting them into its earth and stone, with occasional reminders cresting the surface of its paved streets. It's an ever-growing body, but one that keeps the score. In both films, Cronenberg characterises the city as a place that targets and punishes marginalised characters.

Cronenberg has always been fascinated by how trauma targets the alienated, as an outsider not just to London, but to mainstream Hollywood filmmaking. It is not with nostalgia or sentiment that he operates on London's psyche, but with the grace of a curious and ruthless surgeon. I have been alienated by this city; I have walked its streets feeling like everyone who lives here is communicating on a frequency I am not supposed to know. It's strangely affirming to learn that Cronenberg, an artist of surprising and reliable empathy, isn't convinced London is a space that readily or convincingly welcomes people in.

Spider adapts Patrick McGrath's novel about a schizophrenic man lodging in a halfway house after being released from a psychiatric hospital, placing him in the same area of East London where he spent a difficult childhood. Walking the streets he grew up in, "Spider" (Ralph Fiennes) is violently confronted with his own past, his listless disorientation reflected in the neglected cityscape around him. The bricked-up windows and hollowed-out industrial sites reek of abandonment and no neighbours appear in window frames and doorways – Spider sees in London what he feels inside.

Spider's contemporary narrative is set in the late '80s, after East London's dock industry had collapsed and the region slid into disrepair and poverty. There's little evidence of the efforts to rejuvenate neglected parts of the city in Spider's neighbourhood – what's worse, Spider and London's psyche seem to have been fused. The opening credits show a montage of shabby, partially damaged walls, with patterned, Rorschach-esque stains stretching across their surface. They are markers of decades of distress and pain, with trauma literally absorbed into London's brick and mortar. *Spider*'s psychodrama feels closely tied to the regenerative history of its setting; Cronenberg's film knows that walls and paving cannot forgive or forget – they will remember what people will not.

East London in 2002 is very different to the area in the '80s, but Spider seems barely aware of his present-day surroundings; he's plagued by flashbacks to his impoverished childhood in East London's '60s. Here, his neglectful, abusive father Bill (Gabriel Byrne) has an affair with sex worker Yvonne (Miranda Richardson), eventually murdering Spider's mother (also Richardson) and moving Yvonne into the family home.

Adult Spider makes physical appearances in these flashbacks, illustrating how immersive and lifelike his reflections on the past feel – but crucially adult Spider regularly watches huge sections of his parents' past that he was never present for as a child. This is an invention, a narrative he has constructed, that he nonetheless is unable to leave or look away from. He is trapped in an imagined version of the city.

When he returns to the local pub where his father's infidelity began (a place he visits more in his imagination than in real life), gentrification has clearly made its mark – younger, hipper drinkers sit on picnic benches outside. Even though it looks and feels like a distinct place, Spider still cannot make himself cross the boundary into the pub. Anthropologists have argued that urban renewal has always bought the idea that urban decline can be undone; by externalising London's degradation through Spider's mental health, it's clear how impossible such an idea is. The only place Spider is allowed to belong is within the confines of his irreversible trauma.

Eastern Promises has a more robust narrative than *Spider*, but bodies are still crucial to understanding the extent to which characters are allowed to "belong" in the city. Anna (Naomi Watts) is a British-Russian midwife who obtains a diary belonging to Tatiana (Sarah-Jeanne Labrosse), a sex-trafficked teenage Russian national, after she's admitted to hospital with severe uterine bleeding. She dies giving birth, her child survives, and Anna's search for Tatiana's family leads her to a Russian mafia "vor," Semyon (Armin Mueller-Stahl), who owns a restaurant in central London. His driver, Nikolai (Viggo Mortensen), is entrusted with obtaining and destroying the evidence of Tatiana's trafficking and abuse.

Tatiana appears physically in the film very briefly, but her voice (provided by Tatiana Maslany) appears throughout as a disembodied testimony of exploitation in London, an outsider who was offered none of the protections of citizenship and whose death only happened because of how vulnerable she was inside the city. Her perspective, tinged with a bittersweet hope that London implicitly promised her, stands in stark contrast to Nikolai's; Mortensen's performance ripples with intense, tightly controlled physicality that gives the character a dominating presence in every room he appears.

Tatiana's voice doesn't grant her personhood; she exists only as a record of suffering. Nikolai's body is covered in guarantees of mafia trust and respect, his tattoos spelling out a code of prestige in a secret script. Nikolai is complicated by the reveal that he's an undercover Russian FSB agent, willing to submerge himself in a constructed identity that cuts off the air supply to his humanity. As he tells the Mafia high command: "I died when I was 15. Now I live in the zone all the time." There are people walking London's streets who wield tremendous power – capitalists, gangsters, unempathetic politicians – but in Cronenberg's view, they have no life to them.

Even if the film is less aesthetically grim than *Spider*, the London of *Eastern Promises* is an uglier place; it is a passive host for violent parasites. Cronenberg's dispassionate, severe composition and cold, impactful cuts only embolden the brutality of Semyon's enterprise, visible not only in the unflattering, dank alleys and dark roads but also the trendy, central streets of Barbican where the Trans-Siberian restaurant is located. Each brutal act comes with an unspoken permit granted by a vigilant but unfeeling city.

———

London's status as a collection of disparate, independent zones is underlined by the Russian hierarchies thriving in *Eastern Promises*. Can London call itself inviting, especially to foreign cultures, if it still observes the power dynamics and discriminations held by its most immoral and masochistic inhabitants? In *Eastern Promises*, only violence has been allowed to assimilate and the vulnerable must be content with punishing systems that are condoned by the city's silence. Can you hear it, the voicelessness of London? The neglect, the blind eye, the words kept behind closed doors? Does London's silence sound more like someone strangled, or the strangler?

Of course, any reading of London as, implicitly or explicitly, a mean-spirited place could very easily just be a projection of how an outsider feels having been alienated within. I love the city, but do not feel at home there yet – there are people who have lived there for ten years who feel similarly dispossessed within the city's boundaries. We do not know how at home Cronenberg feels in London, but both *Spider* and *Eastern Promises* feel like they're indulging the outsider's desire to know that something is *wrong* with the city rather than the fact that we do not intimately know its inner workings. Such a desire is perfectly in tune with Cronenberg's motifs of hostile, distressing environments.

Spider is haunted by a disused, deconstructed gasometer, a remnant from deindustrialisation in his East London neighbourhood. The giant, hollow metal frame (formerly the Bethnal Green Gasworks) looms above Spider wherever he goes, like a panopticon casting a piercing spotlight on only the most vulnerable citizens, all while acknowledging him more than any real person in the city. When Spider sits smoking on Regent's Canal, he turns his body away from the structure, as if it can see him, feel him, hurt him. Gasometers are a divisive visual landmark in East London (the one in *Spider* is currently being developed into luxury apartments) but are instantly recognisable to those who've lived in post-industrial spaces. They are themselves ghosts, symbols of labour and actions now forgotten and absent.

For Spider, their symbolic nature is more personal – he has a phobia of gas after, it is revealed, he killed his own mother by gas asphyxiation, believing her to be Yvonne. Without remembering his traumatic crime, the gasometer has a powerful impact on Spider's body, isolating him from reaching clarity or closure. The power of such a character is no doubt due to its recognisability – how many times have you walked past a man like Spider, othering him with simplistic assumptions of how he lives and feels?

I find it easier to navigate London in my dreams. There, I compress the disordered layout of its centralmost streets into a clear path. Where there are gaps in my knowledge, my subconscious will easily skip over, connecting roads and pavements kilometres apart for my convenience. To an outsider, London is most welcoming as an imagined space, one that conforms to their selective knowledge. The reality is overwhelming: the biggest city in the country cannot be tamed or bargained with. To belong there you must meet it on its own terms.

Cronenberg is not considered particularly intimate with London, but the idea of impersonal spaces or entities commanding over individual psyches is right at home in his body of work. London's history, the real and traceable movements of its growth, contrasts with its inherently constructed nature. *This is not a real place*, the outsider screams to themselves. *Then why does it have such a hold on me?* they scream back.

Cronenberg is not interested in the tropes and clichés projected by American or British popular film, but rather what's hidden away; the bodies buried in allotment earth or deposited in optimal points along the Thames. In his duology of the capital, a shifting London is reflected; it wills itself to regenerate while passively regarding all the identities that are shattered, projected, adopted, and reinforced in its wake. *Spider* and *Eastern Promises* colour the city as somewhere where the past, with its poverty, xenophobia, and exploitation, is unreachable, despite its residue staining every surface.

What, or who, will be forgotten here? For Cronenberg, this is not a place of renewal, but of rebirth – rebirth as a taxing, messy, laborious process that can stifle life as much as it can create it. Does "belonging" here mean you are enforcing alienation on those who don't qualify? Holding yourself at a remove from a city that asks too much of outsiders may protect you from losing yourself. But done for long enough, you may find yourself inhabiting, body and soul, a place that won't recognise you. •

LONDON BY OUTSIDERS

01 NIGHT AND THE CITY

1950   dir. Jules Dassin

Weirdo London noir packed to the hilt with sleazy characters whose morals are well and truly in the gutter.

02 THE SERVANT

1963   dir. Joseph Losey

Class warfare classic from US director Losey, with James Fox and Dirk Bogarde as feuding housemates (lovers?).

03 10 RILLINGTON PLACE

1971   dir. Richard Fleischer

Richard Attenborough nails the soft-spoken menace of killer John Christie, whose Notting Hill home doubled as a tomb.

04 THE ELEPHANT MAN

1980   dir. David Lynch

Tackles the life of deformed Joseph Merrick in Victorian London with empathy, sadness, and surrealism.

05 MOONLIGHTING

1984   dir. Jerzy Skolimowski

A heart attack to rival *Uncut Gems*, as a Polish contractor (Jeremy Irons) tries to renovate a London townhouse.

06 I HIRED A CONTRACT KILLER

1990   dir. Aki Kaurismäki

Deadpan comic thriller about a man who regrets hiring a hitman to kill him, shot in London by the Finnish auteur.

07 ABOUT A BOY

2002   dir. Chris Weitz, Paul Weitz

Hugh Grant ditched the floppy locks for this affable rom-com – somehow, it's from the directors of *American Pie*.

08 SPIDER

2002   dir. David Cronenberg

Schizophrenic Ralph Fiennes struggles with reality while trying to survive in a murky East London halfway house.

09 AN EDUCATION

2009   dir. Lone Scherfig

Dane Scherfig captures '60s suburban London in a state of rapid cultural change. Carey Mulligan's breakout.

10 LOST IN LONDON

2017   dir. Woody Harrelson

Harrelson made his directorial debut with this Soho-set curio, a real-time caper originally broadcast live in theatres (a first).

SCREENING THE HEATH

BY LAURA VENNING

One of London's most beloved green spaces offers respite from the grit and the grey. It's a place for thinking and wandering, of inspiration for poets, filmmakers... and critics 'm lucky enough to have always lived within walking distance of Hampstead Heath. Its expansive parkland feels like the only place in the city where I can see the whole sky, and it sits as part of the internal landscape of my memory. If I'm not going for a morning swim with my girlfriend in the Ladies' Pond, I approach the Heath from the east via Fitzroy Park, a steep private road lined by gargantuan houses spanning several eras. Down the hill, past the allotments where sunflowers greet the sky and in winter you might smell a waft of bonfire smoke, turning right where you'll find a pair of golden retrievers snoozing on a small porch in the morning sun, then heading towards the wooded path, you finally stumble left through a patch of mud into meadowland. It's here you can easily deceive yourself into thinking you're in the middle of the countryside, fifty miles from the nearest Pret a Manger.

Since the early nineteenth century, the Heath has been loved as a source of artistic inspiration and communal respite from the relentless noise of central London. An 800-acre expanse of woodland, meadows, playing fields, and swimming ponds four miles north of the Thames, it fulfils the different needs of the many types of people who engage with it. And its function as a cinematic space, whether appearing as itself or playing somewhere else, illuminates its cultural position while reflecting how its visitors spend their time. In 1976's *The Omen*, Gregory Peck – as the American ambassador – takes his Devil-spawn son Damien for a day out on Parliament Hill in the southwest corner of the Heath. The choice of location emphasises the

Heath's function as a space for communal leisure, but one mostly for the upper classes. When a dead body is found on the Heath in Basil Dearden's *Sapphire*, the murder feels shocking for having occured in an affluent area, making the revelation that the victim was "passing" for white more intriguing. Meanwhile, the Heath's role as a substitute for the countryside for city dwellers is made literal in *Monty Python and the Holy Grail*, when the Heath stood in for Scotland in a shot that saw John Cleese's Lancelot storming a castle.

Yet my favourite depiction of the Heath, the one that evokes the wild beauty you'll find if you stray from the well-trodden paths, is in Jane Campion's 2009 film *Bright Star*, the first of her films that I saw, aged sixteen. *Bright Star* is a luminous account of the relationship between Romantic poet John Keats and Fanny Brawne, a young woman who loved reading and became his muse. They lived in adjoining sections of the same house to the southwest of the Heath, now a museum. Their doomed courtship was worthy of any poem: they were engaged but never married because Keats couldn't financially support a family. He died of tuberculosis at age twenty-five, hundreds of miles away in Rome. I was so entranced by Campion's interpretation of their story that it sparked a love for her work that has shaped my career in film criticism. It was my first, transfigurative encounter with cinema's potential as poetry itself, as more than a method of storytelling, as a form that could express deeply felt emotions wordlessly.

I can't claim I've experienced my own divine inspiration in a secluded meadow in the corner of the Heath, just as

Keats did. But that meadow at the end of Fitzroy Park is my favourite area, where the landscape seems wilder and the blackberries sweeter. Here is where I'm most keenly aware of what makes the Heath special; it's a place of communing with nature alongside loved ones, friends, and strangers, at once tactile and transcendent. This area also feels the closest to Campion's vision of the Heath as a sublime space where the intensity of poetry and love are powerful intertwining forces.

Oddly enough, the Heath doesn't actually appear in *Bright Star* as itself. Campion felt that Keats and Fanny's real house was too small and too fusty, so chose to shoot the film in Bedfordshire instead. This seems contradictory – how can my favourite portrayal of a place so constant in my life be shot somewhere else? But Campion, alongside her cinematographer Greig Fraser, capture my experience of the Heath nonetheless (or perhaps they have, in fact, shaped it). They show it as a space where nature is inspiring and healing – think of Keats (Ben Whishaw) cradled by the canopy of a treetop in blossom, or of Fanny (Abbie Cornish) clasping one of her lover's letters and lying on a carpet of bluebells as if embraced by the flowers. The spirit of communal play is here, too – after they share their first kiss by a pond, the couple tease Fanny's little sister by walking behind her, stealing private moments of affection, and then freezing in place every time she turns around. It shatters the perception of the period drama as stuffy and formal, and reminds me of my own adventures on the Heath both as a child and an adult, from summertime scrambling on an enormous fallen tree, to throwing snowballs at my sister, to walking hand in hand with my girlfriend.

Leaving behind that quiet meadow to the east, continue uphill in a north-westerly direction, past clusters of smaller trees where you might encounter a lone hippy placidly tapping a drum in some private ceremony. Cutting a diagonal route across the long grasses, and then down the other side of the windswept slope, you'll meet a rough, shaded path usually thronging with amblers, bikes, dogs, and children. Turn left for the cheerfully basic swimming ponds, right towards Kenwood House.

Kenwood, an eighteenth-century stately home with a clean white facade, exemplifies the perception of Hampstead as a playground for the middle and upper classes, historically and today. The house memorably appears in *Notting Hill* as the filming location for the Henry James adaptation which Anna Scott (Julia Roberts) takes a role in. It also appears in the execrable 2017 romantic comedy *Hampstead*, based loosely on the life of of Harry Hallowes (Brendan Gleeson), who won squatters' rights over his shack on the Heath. Unsurprisingly in this grey pound-courting Harvey Weinstein joint, there's no engagement whatsoever with politics. This film's vision of North London makes Richard Curtis look like Mike Leigh.

But Kenwood was also once home to Dido Elizabeth Belle, the biracial daughter of a Black female slave and a British naval officer, played by Gugu Mbatha-Raw in the 2013 biopic *Belle*, directed by Amma Asante. Adopted by her great uncle William Murray, 1st Earl of Mansfield and Lord Chief Justice, she lived a life of luxury, though she was never truly accepted in society due to both her race and her illegitimacy. A portrait of Dido and her adopted sister Elizabeth is unique in British art of the time, as it shows the women as almost equal, though the pale and blonde Elizabeth is in the foreground.

Dido's story is a stark reminder of the violent histories of some stately homes and of the riches made from the slave trade coming down through the generations to those who still live in the exorbitantly expensive Hampstead and Highgate. Kenwood House is now free to access, and its collection includes paintings by masters like Vermeer and Rembrandt. It's a gift to Londoners and contributes to the Heath as a community space, but one that remains tethered to a colonial past. I was taken to Kenwood countless times as a child; I can visualise each painting and walk through its elegant halls in my mind, sensing every creak in the floorboards. Before Asante's film, I was naive to Kenwood's bloody politics, but the knowledge still impacts every visit.

Turning away from Kenwood now, going back down the hill towards the east side on a shaded path, you'll find the single-gender swimming ponds, a place of more subversive encounters. Here is a different sense of the Heath as a communal space: both ponds have been sites of connection for queer Londoners for decades. In the summer, my girlfriend and I have joined the women sunbathing topless in the adjoining meadow, free from leering, soundtracked by splashes and laughter. Men admire each other on the grass next to the Men's Pond; it's both a cruising spot and an area for homosocial bonding. Gary Oldman's George Smiley in *Tinker Tailor Soldier Spy* epitomises the British establishment by swimming in the Mixed Pond on the opposite side of the Heath, avoiding any queer connotations.

Filmmaker, artist, and patron saint of queer Britain Derek Jarman chronicled his time cruising on Hampstead Heath in his diaries, published three years before he died of AIDS-related illness in 1994. "On warm nights the drunken scent of the May caresses lovers under the sighing trees of Hampstead Heath," he once wrote. Such a line could almost be from a Keats poem. A year before his death, Jarman appeared in a short film directed by Alexis Bistikas entitled *The Clearing*, following a journey through a wooded area of the Heath known as a spot for cruising. The camera takes on the perspective of a wanderer lured by the sound of a saxophone. The wanderer encounters various figures: a pretty young man eyes him while smoking, a huddle of men surrounds one clad in leather, another in a gimp suit, a boy in a school uniform offers him an apple. When we reach the saxophonist in the clearing the wanderer is revealed to be Jarman himself, gazing at the player with lust, then with a kind of profound melancholy. It's a psychoanalytic journey into what could be Jarman's own conflicting memories and desires; cruising as an act of resistance against repressive heterosexual society. Bistikas would himself die of AIDs-related illness in 1995; the film acts as an elegy for both men. Perhaps *The Clearing*, poetic in itself, is not as far removed as it may seem from *Bright Star* – both tell stories about brilliant men whose lives were cut tragically short by disease, who wandered the Heath in search of inspiration or the joy of brief connection.

Continuing to wander onwards, then, as Derek Jarman

once did, for our final stretch: west past Parliament Hill, across the bridge overlooking the Mixed Pond to the edge of the Heath. Left onto South End Road, past the turning to Downshire Hill, as you might notice the dome of St. John's Church, where my parents were married, and then, on your right, that unassuming road is Keats Grove, where the real John Keats and Fanny Brawne lived. At the end of *Bright Star*, Fanny, heavy with grief at the news of Keats' death, walks through the snow-blanketed woodlands of the Heath and as night draws in she recites Keats' sonnet "Bright star, would I were stedfast as thou art," an ode to eternal love which he dedicated to her. Here, Campion keeps the camera's gaze fixed on Fanny's face in all its devastation, as she speaks the words that have become immortal. It recalls Jarman's expression at the end of *The Clearing*.

My relationship with the Heath has changed; in the third UK lockdown, it was a place I went to to try to temper my own sense of despair. When depression took hold, I'd retread the same paths, no end in sight and no poetic inspiration to be found. But, just as spring returns, unbelievable as it seems every year, so the Heath quietly bloomed into a place I could take refuge in again. In going on this meander, I wasn't expecting to find a kinship, however loose, between Jarman and Keats. In recognising this link, I feel that I'm uniting what feel like disparate parts of myself: the child taken on walks, the shy teenager drawn to the cinema, particularly the films of Jane Campion, as a means of articulating feelings I couldn't express, and the openly queer woman I am today. None of the films I've mentioned have really captured everything the Heath is and means to me and its thousands of other visitors. Maybe that's the point. Yet in considering its life on screen, I've come to understand a little bit more about the place where I grew up, the place I still live in, and the person I always was but am still becoming. •

LOVE & LUST IN LONDON

01 INDISCREET

1958   dir. Stanley Donen

During posh London dates, Ingrid Bergman falls for Cary Grant – a bachelor with a habit for bending the truth.

02 MY BEAUTIFUL LAUNDRETTE

1985   dir. Stephen Frears

Daniel Day-Lewis (with two-tone hair!) runs a laundrette with his Pakistani lover (Gordon Warnecke) in '80s London.

03 THE END OF THE AFFAIR

1999   dir. Neil Jordan

Glimpse the Phoenix Cinema (one of London's oldest) in this swooning adaptation of Graham Greene's great novel.

04 NOTTING HILL

1999   dir. Roger Michell

Inaccurate but irresistible fable about a Notting Hill bookshop owner who falls in love with Julia Roberts.

05 CLOSER

2004   dir. Mike Nichols

The lives of four individuals overlap in Mike Nichols' sexy romantic drama, with a key part for Postman's Park.

06 BRIGHT STAR

2009   dir. Jane Campion

Abbie Cornish and Ben Whishaw swoon amid lush springtime scenery in this tale about Romantic poet John Keats.

07 THE DEEP BLUE SEA

2011   dir. Terence Davies

Achingly romantic and woozily sad drama about a housewife's affair with a handsome RAF pilot; tissues at the ready.

08 PHANTOM THREAD

2017   dir. Paul Thomas Anderson

PTA's austere drama, set within the '50s London fashion scene, is as handsomely mounted as it is increasingly strange.

09 THE SOUVENIR

2019   dir. Joanna Hogg

Hogg's autobiographical grappling with the sad romance of her film student youth, set in '80s Knightsbridge.

10 RYE LANE

2023   dir. Raine-Anne Miller

Spotlight on Peckham in this lovely, infectious jaunt – an antidote to the so-often watered-down London of cinema.

THE GARDEN

BY TOM BARNARD

Grappling with grief, encounters with two films – *The Boy and the Heron* and *All of Us Strangers* – form an oddly timely path for a writer in London looking to heal

I am seated on a plush, red sofa at the Everyman Muswell Hill. In four days, my mum will die. The film I'm here to see, unbeknownst to me, is a portrait of grief set during the Second World War, about a young boy who loses his mother during the American bombing of Japan. To cope, he escapes into a fantasy world to process his feelings of loss and abandonment.

It's the latest film from Japanese animator Hayao Miyazaki, one of my favourite filmmakers. I have avoided the trailers and plot outlines during the build-up to the film's release as to go in blind, and have even insisted – probably to the irritation of others – on calling the movie by its original, more poetic Japanese title, *How Do You Live?*, rather than the more generic Western alternative: *The Boy and the Heron.*

But I've been caught out: my bid to avoid the finer details of the movie beforehand has backfired. For just over two hours, I find it impossible to concentrate on Miyazaki's admittedly frenetic meditation on death, not only because of the two young boys nattering in the front row (*well*, I think, *at least they've come out to see a foreign movie!*), but the deep feelings the movie drags up. Feelings I have been trying to repress.

Afterwards, I step into the chilly December air, eyes drawn to the glowing shopfronts of Muswell Hill bakeries and food stores in the fading light. The movie doesn't work, I declare. A misfire. A disappointment!

What a shame, given this will probably be Miyazaki's last-ever feature.

And I'd been waiting for so long to see it.

A month earlier, in late November, I attend a preview screening and Q&A for Andrew Haigh's romantic drama *All of Us Strangers* at the Curzon Mayfair, a film I am told in advance is "excellent," but of which I know very little about. In the lobby, I chat with fellow film writers (two of whom will go on to write essays for this very book). One writer tells me she has already seen the film three times.

Having walked through Christmassy Mayfair, adorned with twinkling lights and oversized fir trees, I chat idly, sipping free beer, feeling happy with my lot – the perfect prerequisite for a world about to turn upside down. A call comes through then – the unusual timing of which tells me that something bad has happened. I slip outside, passing the film's grinning star, Paul Mescal, who shoots me a friendly smile, though I'm too anxious to be starstruck (all I can think is: *he is smaller than I imagined*). The person on the end of the phone tells me my mum's condition has worsened. She is very ill and has gone into hospital. I should think seriously about flying to Spain, where she lives, the next day.

I wander back to the lobby in a daze, having walked a mile around the streets of Westminster on autopilot, heart thumping in my chest. I try to calm down. Not much I can do right now, so I will attempt to enjoy the movie (in retrospect, a ridiculous delusion). As I sit waiting for the film to start, my partner, also in attendance and having listened to what I have to say, turns to me with a look of apprehension. "You know this is about Dead Parents, right?" I attempt a laugh, but it is a nervous, unconvincing laugh. In truth, I feel sick. A Dead Parents movie is the last thing I need. I brace for impact, but end up excusing myself and leaving just as the lights begin to dim.

The next day, I do fly to Spain – though she does not pass. A short period of false hope follows (I lie to myself: *maybe it will be okay*), but the dreaded thing seems inevitable, any day now, just a matter of time. It eventually does happen, two months later, four days after that viewing of *The Boy and the Heron* – and on New Year's Eve, no less, a few hours before midnight (if there is such a thing as an awkward time to die, maybe that is it). I am two drinks in at a friend's house when the call comes through.

Back to Spain, then. The airport. The empty roads. The funeral. Grief.

I Google synonyms for grief, fearful of overusing the word in this essay. And yet there seems to be no other word that feels quite fit for purpose – no other that is recognised and associated with loss in the same way. Misery, sorrow, pain… they do not quite capture the same feeling of emotional weight. Grief suggests longevity, *a working through*, I think, that the other words do not encompass. Misery, sorrow, and pain can be fixed: grief is perpetual.

In the days right after, when the world expects you to just plough on, nowhere feels right. Imagine my surprise, then, when I find I am glad to be back in London, in spite of the shitty weather, the busyness. Spain is too quiet, gives you too much space to think; I feel better being somewhere loud and uncompromising, where the sound of my thoughts can be drowned out by the rattling of Tube carriages, the terrible Ed Sheeran buskers in Leicester

Square, the indifference of nine million others who choose to call this city home.

But I am grateful, too, for another reason, one I would not have expected under the circumstances. More than anything, I find myself craving escape into dark, semi-occupied rooms at odd times of day. The cinemas of London, it turns out, are the ideal fit for my inner turmoil to play out. That strange desire to be alone, but not entirely alone, perfectly attended to by a random one o'clock screening on a Thursday afternoon. So I see *In the Mood for Love*, and *Chungking Express*, which seem to play on an endless loop at the Prince Charles Cinema – comfort movies, in a way, not because they're easy watches, but in their depiction of lives so distant and so removed from my own.

January. It's around this time that I start to see the posters going up. The giant faces of Andrew Scott and Paul Mescal are everywhere I look. Emails in my inbox: invites to more preview screenings, requests to interview the cast. I see these and – quickly, childishly – close my browser window, thinking "leave me alone!" *All of Us Strangers*, all of the time – not to mention the verbal adoration spewing from friends, family, and peers, calling it one of the best and most moving films they've ever seen. London, then, true to form, set to play tormentor and saviour in equal measure; a city primed to ease my grief and also to exacerbate it.

The film becomes a kind of albatross, though credit where credit's due: I have rarely seen a British film advertised and marketed with as much force and conviction as this one. Before every movie I see at the cinema, I am ambushed by the trailer, blasted with the Pet Shop Boys' cover of "Always on My Mind." In my own mind, the song begins to feel like a personal attack. My reaction to hearing about the movie is thrown all out of proportion, something to remind me of what I am trying to avoid and quash down. A London bus goes past, the film's title moving in my eyeline; the sight of it hits me like a slap in the face.

Strangely, in the weeks after, I begin to imagine the foundations of a short story in which a son returns to an empty house where his deceased parent once lived, only to find said parent still living there – a ghostly apparition occupying the space, no idea they've died. In a bid to avoid his pain, the son ignores the supernatural entity and chooses instead to buy into the fantasy: him, refusing to let go; the ghost, refusing to acknowledge their illness. "A bit like *All of Us Strangers*, then," a friend tells me as we wait for a train at the dystopian hell that is Euston station.

I blink. "That's the plot?"

"Well, kind of. Wait, you haven't seen it?"

The Piccadilly line, rising to street level from the endless escalators at Holborn station. Out into the freezing rain. This winter seems to have lasted forever, stretching into springtime. I glance at hooded protesters assembled on the corner of Gate Street, fighting a cause but also the relentlessness of the weather. I don't mind the regular downpours right now, though, maybe even relish them: the way they generate a mood that demands you find somewhere to hole up. The rain, after all, gives a person permission to hide.

I take refuge in an overpriced café to work on this very book, when – of course – I come across those four gut-wrenching words in one of the essays I'm editing: "*All of Us Strangers.*" I can't help but laugh at the timing: no escape, months later, they always seem to find me. There has been a feeling this week, more than any other in memory, of the oppressiveness of London; the way it can flatten you, force you into a race you have no chance of winning. Rising costs, lowering standards. But I've also started to dream of walking the chaotic, tuk-tuk-packed streets of Bangkok, of the hustle and bustle of a Delhi market, of places louder and even more crushing on the senses than the city where I live – a promise of relief by way of sheer overstimulation.

Walking without purpose, moving now for the sake of moving, past empty pubs, vape shops, and hollowed-out shopfronts, I stop and look around, recognising the street but not quite knowing why. I linger for a second and discover I am outside The Garden Cinema. The Garden, one of London's newest independent cinemas, where I have inhaled a history of great cinema, from *New York, New York* (drunk on four negronis) to *Picnic at Hanging Rock* (sober, and probably for the best).

I'm hoping, by way of some spectacular luck, that something good – something long and immersive – is about to begin, a three-hour classic I've never gotten around to seeing with the potential to whisk me away. But of course, it is not *The Great Escape* that's playing (one day I will watch you), but *All of Us Strangers* – months after its initial release, and starting in less than fifteen minutes.

But this time, for some reason, my instinct isn't to flinch.

Instead I find myself moving inside, not thinking too much, buying a ticket from the front desk ("Last one," I'm told), before descending the staircase to the basement, into the Art Deco-inspired bar. The attendant there turns to me. "What can I get you?"

I ask for a Coke.

"Sure thing," he says. A pause, then: "So, what are you seeing?"

"*All of Us Strangers*," I tell him, though I can barely get the words out. Then, alluding to the fact that it has been out for a while, "I know, I'm a bit late to the party."

He looks down, filling a glass with ice, and nods. "You're okay," he says, misunderstanding me, "it hasn't started yet."

Screen 2 is smaller, but my preferred screen at The Garden. I take my usual seat, on the aisle, so I can hang my legs out, three rows from the front. A feeling overcomes me as I sit through the trailers – one I haven't felt since *Indiana Jones and the Dial of Destiny* (though for very different reasons): I am nervous.

Somehow the journey here, a journey through my own anxieties, through the streets of the city, through some really, really strange coincidences, seems to have coalesced in a final destination of my own making. Am I simply a glutton for punishment, putting myself through this at what feels like my lowest point? But it's too late to think about it now; the lights are going down.

It can be tempting to draw connections between things in life that aren't really there. But maybe it's important to lean into them, too, when they are powering a narrative of recovery. In other words: sometimes you watch something, in the right place, at the right time, when you really need to. What the film meant, or said to me, on that random afternoon at The Garden, probably matters less than the notion that I simply went to see it. Yet to say that *All of Us Strangers*, in that viewing, "spoke to me," doesn't quite cut it.

The film, in so many ways, seems pulled out of my own experiences. Andrew Scott's grieving writer Adam, walking the empty, eerie suburban streets where I actually grew up, passing on the tracks and through the parks of my youth. Snatches of a childhood that could have been taken from my own: train rides through East Croydon station; Saturdays spent at the (then-resplendent, now decrepit) Whitgift Centre; the mention of family holidays to Disneyland in Florida. All of these things, I did – at one time or another – with my own mum.

What resonates, too, is its depiction of a more liminal, ethereal London. The London where people hide in soulless tower blocks, seeking solace for fear of making a genuine connection; the city as a lonely place, rather than a hectic one, where life is not experienced in lively pubs, but put on pause. I, too, had been using London to hide – only my tower block was an 11:30am showing of *The Enigma of Kaspar Hauser* in a half-empty screen at the BFI. Cinema, as a space for both solace and confrontation. But isn't London, too? Slowly, the narrative in *All of Us Strangers* gives way, transforming Adam's listless worldview into one of quiet understanding.

It turns out the reasons why I had tried so desperately to avoid this film were the exact reasons I needed to see it. As I step out into the rain afterwards, I feel a rush of catharsis, the way you do when you finally tell a friend something that has been playing on your mind. The realisation of another person's pain, even a fictional person, eases my own. I learn from my phone that director Andrew Haigh, like me, grew up in Croydon. I stand on the pavement, feeling exposed – but also slightly lighter on my feet.

Around me, the 5 o'clock rush reaches its apex: city workers, tourists, a stag do of intoxicated Northerners making a beeline for the next pub. Across the street, a tall woman dressed in orange is yelling something about the war, though I am not sure which one. Catching my studied expression, maybe, a homeless man camped outside Sainsbury's leans up towards me, and – lost in my head – I prepare to dismiss him. But he only asks, "You alright, mate?"

London, I think, *reaching out in unexpected ways.*

The Sunday afterwards is Mother's Day. In her absence, it's unclear how to go about things. Then it comes to me, what I must do, out of nowhere, the only thing that seems right. I must face not an albatross, but another demonic bird, the one voiced by Robert Pattinson in the English dub – haunting me ever since I first encountered him in Muswell Hill.

I see *The Boy and the Heron* again, almost three months after I first let the entire thing fly over my head. That day, viewed alone, free of the anxiety of impending disaster, I appreciate its complicated vision more. My initial bid to write it off as a misfire seems misguided; instead I feel Miyazaki's deep sadness, his grappling with the inevitable grief that comes with existing in a world where things are often out of our control. But also there, in the ending, a kind of affirmation of life from somebody who has lived honestly; a message to grow and move forward; a sincere acceptance of one's responsibilities as a human being.

I head home, and – sitting with yet another film I realised I was hiding from – feel something in me is made different. That same evening, thousands of miles away in Los Angeles, *The Boy and the Heron* wins the Oscar for Best Animated Feature, further cementing the strange connections running through this essay; connections that, all along, I have perhaps pulled together in a bid to give shape to my grief in the only way I know how.

I remember the film's original title, *How Do You Live?*, and prepare to make my way through. •

SOUTH LONDON

01 UP THE JUNCTION

1968   dir. Ken Loach

Classic kitchen sink drama about a wealthy heiress who trades her privilege for a new life in working class Battersea.

02 ENTERTAINING MR. SLOANE

1970   dir. Douglas Hickox

Orton's wild play of murder and nymphomania takes in the districts of Brockley, East Dulwich, and Camberwell.

03 JUBILEE

1978   dir. Derek Jarman

Queen Elizabeth I travels 400 years into the future to find punks causing havoc in Southwark and Deptford.

04 THE FIRM

1989   dir. Alan Clarke

Gary Oldman terrifies as a maniacal estate agent who's also a football hooligan. A South-East London classic.

05 NIL BY MOUTH

1997   dir. Gary Oldman

Gary Oldman's one and only directorial credit is a banger; a working class drama that leaves a taste like an ashtray.

06 GOODBYE CHARLIE BRIGHT

2001   dir. Nick Love

Plenty of urban grit in this South London tale, as two friends find their bond tested during a long, hot summer.

07 TREACLE JR.

2010   dir. Jamie Thraves

In the midst of a mid-life crisis, a dad becomes purposefully homeless in the environs of Dulwich and Peckham.

08 HONEYTRAP

2014   dir. Rebecca Johnson

Brixton-set tale based on the true story of a young girl who lures an infatuated lover into a violent trap.

09 ALL OF US STRANGERS

2023   dir. Andrew Haigh

A lonely screenwriter navigates liminal London and the Croydon of his childhood in this moving, eerie ghost story.

10 HOARD

2023   dir. Luna Carmoon

Intense debut about a girl whose stinky upbringing influences her feral teenage years, set on a Lewisham estate.

Inter

mission

PORTOBELLO ROADS

BY LEILA LATIF

It's the most famous street in London's most famous neighbourhood (thanks, Richard Curtis). But has cinema really done right by the reality of Portobello Road?

was six years old when I realised I wanted to live in Notting Hill. That I *needed* to live in Notting Hill. This plan was set in stone all the way back in 1992, the same year that Frank Crichlow of the Mangrove Nine was awarded £50,000 in damages from the Metropolitan Police after a sustained campaign of terror against him and his Notting Hill restaurant, The Mangrove.

My reasons were not as noble as wanting to be speaking truth to power at the heart of Black British activism, but a 10-minute musical segment in the 1971 Disney film *Bedknobs and Broomsticks*. For those who haven't seen it, the film is set in 1940 during the Blitz and follows three orphans who leave London to stay in Dorset with Miss Eglantine Price (Angela Lansbury), who is undertaking lessons in witchcraft to help in the British fight against the enemy. She and the children team up with Professor Emelius Browne (David Tomlinson) to find the second half of a spellbook, and there is only one place to go when you need absolutely anything – Notting Hill's iconic Portobello Road.

In a film packed with fantastical whimsy, nothing seemed more magical to six-year-old me than the road itself. Lightly shabby but brimming with charm, the characters sang about how it is a "street where the riches of ages are stowed" and how "a lady will always feel dressed à la mode in frillies she finds in the Portobello Road." The children breathe in "London's lovely sooty air," and the street is filled with all the joys of life. There's a distinctly working-class community at play and one accepting of all kinds of people.

They dance to the Caribbean steel drums and Scottish bagpipes. They perform Irish jigs, and Sikh soldiers in turbans steal the show with their acrobatic efforts. Even though I suspected eating whelks out of an unrefrigerated wheelbarrow was probably a bad idea, I knew I wanted to one day find my way to that wondrous street to do just that.

Notting Hill drastically changed after the Blitz. The area around Portobello was devastated, leaving huge pockets of bomb-damaged buildings. It became popular with the Windrush generation as the rents were cheap and the transport links were decent. Still, much of it degraded into the slum housing that photographer Roger Mayne famously documented in 1956, taking photographs of Southam Street, where people lived in derelict Victorian terrace houses. Those houses would later be demolished to create Ernő Goldfinger's brutalist modern council building, the Trellick Tower, at the very top of Portobello, where flats can now go for a million pounds – and only 500 yards from where Crichlow's restaurant once stood.

The steel drums the Caribbean soldiers play as women in quadrilles sway their hips now feels like the nexus of the Notting Hill Carnival, which began in 1959 and to this day celebrates Caribbean food, music, and dance each August Bank Holiday weekend. When *Bedknobs and Broomsticks* came out, the event (always referred to as just "carnival" by locals) consisted of the Russell Henderson Combo and Selwyn Baptiste's Notting Hill Adventure Playground Steelband, and only 500 dancing spectators; today it tops two million annual attendees.

While Portobello Road had changed, as London did in

the decades that followed, in Steve McQueen's *Mangrove* we meet it at the point of a seismic transformation. McQueen has described his historical drama as a "West London western." There's the reluctant anti-hero in the form of Crichlow (Shaun Parkes), who has a colourful past but just now wants to settle down in peace, the dastardly sheriff (Sam Spruell) who just won't let him move on, alongside the young, idealistic gunslinger Darcus Howe (Malachi Kirby), an activist and journalist who wants to stand up to the cruelty his community faces. Notting Hill becomes the frontier for the Black settlers defending themselves against unfriendly natives, and in classic western form, the community must play by its own rules, with personal justice taking moral precedence over formal institutions of law.

In less abstract terms, the film is the story of the Mangrove Nine, named as such because of their ties to Frank Crichlow's Notting Hill restaurant. The restaurant and its Black patrons are subjected to a racist reign of terror by the local police led by Constable Pulley. In 1970 they marched in a peaceful protest from The Mangrove restaurant at the northern end of Portobello Road to the Notting Hill Police Station at its southern tip, chanting "Hands off Black people!" only to discover the police ready to brutalise them. When charged with "riot and affray" the nine men and women faced trial at the Old Bailey, where they were eventually found innocent in the first legal acknowledgement of racist police brutality in the UK.

As the film commences, we see a very different Portobello

Road than the one where Angela Lansbury danced a Scottish jig. Frank Crichlow walks to his restaurant and most of the people he passes by are Black, most of the graffiti is racist, and children clamber over decades-old bombed-out patches of land in makeshift playgrounds. Above the Victorian terrace houses, two large structures are being built alongside Portobello. One is the Westway, which would link the area more speedily to the centre of town, making it all the more desirable a space, and the other is Grenfell Tower, which I would watch burn from my window while clutching my 6-month-old daughter on a dreadful 2017 morning. That day, it felt like every person in Notting Hill walked down Portobello Road overwhelmed and bonded by grief, most laden with everything they could carry to hand to the survivors. That community of different people from all over the world coming together in unison, just like in *Bedknobs and Broomsticks*, was back.

Because the truth of the matter is that the movies had lied to me, and community was about more than just facing a tragedy as one. I can see now that by the time I finally got to move to Notting Hill in my 20s, the golden period was well and truly over. A walk down Portobello still had its charms, but as in 1999's Richard Curtis romantic comedy *Notting Hill*, you were more likely to bump into a bumbling Etonian with a movie star girlfriend than swallow down a whelk as people danced in the street. One of the most popular urban legends that Notting Hill residents tell themselves is that the film was actually part of an elaborate property development scheme; that Richard Curtis wanted to sell his house just off Portobello and figured that a romantic comedy named after the area would boost its price on the market.

The film itself is about a bookshop owner (Hugh Grant) living on Portobello Road and falling in love with a glamorous American movie star (Julia Roberts) who is in town to shoot a film. We are led to believe that these two gorgeous, cishet, privileged white people and their love story face a near insurmountable cultural divide which, to give Grant and Roberts credit, they sell with reasonable aplomb. Despite my own reservations, the romantic comedy is beloved by millions and meant that when any non-Londoner asked where I lived, my response was always met with a nod of approval. Post-Curtis' film, the area's popularity surged. In 1999, the average house in the area cost around £300,000. Today, it's over £1.5 million and many of the independent businesses and working-class residents have been forced out.

Hugh Grant's character, William Thacker, owns a travel bookshop on 142 Portobello itself (famously, the one with the blue door). A surefire way to infuriate any Notting Hill resident is to ask about this bookshop, as hundreds of people queue up each day to take photos outside *an entirely unrelated bookshop on Blenheim Crescent,* which just painted itself blue as a way to get the tourists in. 142 Portobello has also gone down an equally cynical route. It still has a sign saying "The Travel Bookshop" above it (also infuriating, since the film's bookshop is technically called "The Travel Book Company"). It has a large poster of Julia Roberts in the window and sells charmless, mass-produced tat at inflated prices. It had once been a real bookshop, opened and run by a family from 1979 until the area's rising rents meant it had to close in 2011, the same year I moved to Notting Hill.

The irony of Richard Curtis's film being part of gentrifying out his own protagonist's business is not lost on me. But even in 2011, his depiction of all that surrounded Portobello didn't match what I saw with my own two eyes. Frank Crichlow had died a Notting Hill resident and beloved icon the previous year, but the area was still way more diverse than Curtis had made it out to be. There was a sense that, while the best times were behind this area, there was still enough clinging on to make it worthwhile, and it became a kind of microcosm of the three films, with working-class London, Windrush descendants, and poshos with floppy hair all having a seat at the table.

But nearly a decade later, when Steve McQueen's *Mangrove* was released in 2020, the foundational rot in that uneasy détente had been exposed. Portobello now ran down the wealthiest borough in the city, with the average income per head three times that of the national average. There is a blue plaque at the former site of The Mangrove commemorating Frank Crichlow, but it's hard to make out given its position by the 1st-floor window of a restaurant painted the same shade of blue, which sells £20 burgers and £15 cocktails. When the whelk-eating child from *Bedknobs and Broomsticks* sang "you can eat like a king on Portobello Road!", that was now only true if your bank account resembled that of a king, too. And that was the world that led to the Grenfell tragedy, where working-class people had been incinerated by combustible cladding, shoved onto a building to make their homes look more palatable to the gentrifying masses.

Mangrove (which I believe to be Steve McQueen's best film) shows us how those events were set in motion and eulogises what this place used to be. Shaun Parkes, as a happy but slightly weary Frank Crichlow standing outside The Mangrove, saying "This we home," while listening to the same steel drums Lansbury danced to. The acquittal of the Mangrove Nine and the release of *Bedknobs and Broomsticks* both occurring in 1971 feels serendipitous. Echoes of West Indian music seem to travel through space and time and bring disparate people together to the same beat. Even if Richard Curtis saw Portobello Road as a place where Hugh Grant's break-ups were the greatest source of anguish, he failed to capture just how much more it has meant, and continues to mean, to the many people, and peoples, who once marched down it.

Portobello Road would appear in other films, of course: social realism detective tale *The Blue Lamp*, absurd spy comedy *Otley*, and the much-loved *Paddington* films, the last of which would see Hugh Grant return to the now travel bookshop-less street. And I moved a mile north to a distinctly less cinematic patch of London between Kilburn and Queen's Park. But I still go back to Portobello Road all the time. There are still a few great antique shops, some decent pubs, and a wonderful cinema that has been there since 1911 and even survived the Blitz. Every August bank holiday, I strap on my comfiest trainers, eat jerk chicken, listen to steel drums, and dance to grime-blasting sound systems on the streets with a can of room-temperature

Red Stripe that some entrepreneurial young fellow has sold me out of a wheelbarrow. But I don't recognise the magical place I saw when I was six and so desperately wanted to live in. Portobello Road is still a bustling, vibrant part of the city, but *my* Portobello now exists only in the movies. •

BLACK LIVES IN LONDON

01 PRESSURE

1976   dir. Horace Ové

The UK's first Black dramatic feature-length film; a key, impassioned text about systemic racism and Windrush.

02 BLACK JOY

1977   dir. Anthony Simmons

A series of gaffes befall an immigrant in this witty, charismatic comedy; comes with an iconic soul/R&B soundtrack.

03 BABYLON

1980   dir. Franco Rosso

Pulsing reggae beats underscore this pioneering tale about discrimination against the Black community in '70s London.

04 BURNING AN ILLUSION

1981   dir. Menelik Shabazz

Love and self-realization in Ladbroke Grove, as a Black woman finds her voice in '80s London.

05 PLAYING AWAY

1987   dir. Horace Ové

Cultural clash on the cricket pitch: Brixton locals go up against a posh rural team in this comic gem.

06 BABYMOTHER

1998   dir. Julian Henriques

Reggae rhythms in Harlesden in a vibrant tale of a mother chasing her dancehall dreams; the first Black British musical.

07 A MOVING IMAGE

2016   dir. Shola Amoo

Art and activism intersect as a filmmaker explores Brixton gentrification, capturing the city's shifting landscape.

08 BEEN SO LONG

2018   dir. Tinge Krishnan

Michaela Coel-starring musical about a single mum who falls for an an ex-con; doubles as a love letter to Camden.

09 SMALL AXE (TV ANTHOLOGY SERIES)

2020   dir. Steve McQueen

Five remarkable, standalone films about London's West Indian community, set between the late '60s and the mid-'80s.

10 PRETTY RED DRESS

2022   dir. Dionne Edwards

A red dress serves as a symbol of gender tension in South London, set to the songs of Tina Turner.

THE WORD

BY EMILY MASKELL

A space for queer literature that doubles as a community hub, Gay's the Word had a starring role in the film *Pride*. Today, this bookshop is as important as ever

Whenever I get gloomy about the state of the world, I think about Gay's the Word, the quaint, independent bookshop halfway down Marchmont Street in London's bustling district of Bloomsbury, home to hundreds of stories united by a common theme: their connection to the LGBTQ+ community.

Stepping into the bookshop, and being welcomed with the chime of a bell and the light rustle of turning pages, is like returning to a home away from home. Sunlight shines through the shopfront and the warmth hits your back like a guiding hand, as you make your way past Progress Pride flags lining the walls, bookshelves overflowing with tales old and new, real and imagined, from fiction to memoirs, history, and poetry. Here, stories linger not merely in the colourful book spines, but within the space itself.

Gay's the Word was founded in 1979. From the beginning, it was never just a shop, but a community hub. Set up by members of the socialist LGBTQ+ group Gay Icebreakers at a time when gay books weren't widely available, the space cemented itself as a location crucial to London's queer culture. Several LGBTQ+ groups have found their home in Gay's the Word, including TransLondon and the Lesbian Discussion Group, the latter of which continues to host regular meetings in the bookshop. People have walked through its doors for decades, just as the shop has weathered homophobic hate crimes, the rise of Amazon, threats, and raids. Despite it all, Gay's the Word stands as a proud, prevailing, and focal LGBTQ+ monolith in the capital.

It was at the crossroads of cinema and queer history that I first stumbled across Gay's the Word. Before I lived in London, the bookshop shot straight to the top of my "must-visit list" after a viewing of Matthew Warchus' 2014 historical comedy-drama *Pride*. The acclaimed film recounts how a London-based gay and lesbian activist group, Lesbians and Gays Support the Miners (LGSM), founded by the late Mark Ashton, fundraised to support Welsh miners during the strike of 1984 against Margaret Thatcher's government. In *Pride*, this historical moment is revisited with an abundance of colour and plenty of comedic flair. At the heart of LGSM's operation was their headquarters: Gay's the Word. The bookshop plays a seminal role in the film not only as a cosy meeting spot but an embodiment of determined, persevering queerness.

Pride opens with a scene set at London's 1984 Gay Pride March. Loud chants and Pride banners cut through the capital's inherent greyness, while onlookers spout heckles in their direction. After a day of protest, the celebration continues with a house party, but there's something that lingers in the mind of Mark (Ben Schnetzer). He leads a small crowd out the door and into the glorious neighbouring bookshop, Gay's the Word, and announces he's creating an alliance to support the National Union of Mineworkers. The bookshop we see on screen, however, is not the real brick-and-mortar place of the present day. With some movie magic, Warchus recreated the bookshop's '80s appearance, café area, and noticeboards with accurate posters, flyers, and badge replicas, with books from the shop's own secondhand section lining the shelves. It is here

Pride shows how the blueprint of unexpected solidarity begins to take shape. Through *Pride*, I was able to see Gay's the Word as though frozen in time. This glimpse at a place I'd never visited, and people that I never knew, somehow felt achingly familiar. With decades separating them and now, it's the space's warm glow, stacked shelves, and prevalent inclusivity which continues to lure in visitors from near and far.

Jim MacSweeney, a "voracious reader" and the soft-spoken, ever-welcoming manager of Gay's the Word since 1989, recalls that the bookshop has "always been about ideas and making connections first." From the '80s, all the way to now, MacSweeney tells me that "the bookshop hasn't integrally changed that much. It's always been a friendly and community-orientated space." MacSweeney has a large part to play in that: he is never without a great book recommendation and has continued the bookshop's foundations of acceptance. The same inviting aura is also glimpsed in *Pride*, as viewers are beckoned into the inner LGSM circle as if we, too, were participating in these member meetings. The camera is placed at eye level as Ashton calls for solidarity in a spot where you can still stand, his words echoing from the past, ricocheting between the shelves. Watching the film, I felt a sense of community that, as a closeted teen over a hundred miles away, I longed for but felt so disconnected from in my own life. I became emotionally invested not only in the characters of *Pride*, but the charming bookshop that symbolised a place of unity. That sentiment still remains true.

When I first stepped through the doors of Gay's the Word,

it felt like a quiet coming-out. I browsed the bookshelves in what would now constitute part of a relaxed weekend stroll. At the time, the act felt terrifyingly revolutionary. The quiet hums and whispers soundtracked a new realisation: that I was now surrounded by stories reflecting my own truth. In a film about my life, this would be a seminal coming-of-age moment. Before I was out to anyone, it was a place where I would return. I went with friends, and then my parents, in what was an unspoken attempt to flag my own queerness. Then, once I'd moved to London, the bookshop morphed into a place I'd take friends who were visiting and a regular spot where I'd go for evening book talks. I became unable to walk Marchmont Street without sticking my head through the doorway and adding another paperback to my growing to-be-read stack.

What started as apprehension soon turned to deep adoration, and I know I'm not alone in the experience of growth through self-acceptance. This arc is captured brilliantly in *Pride*, through the character of closeted student Joe "Bromley" Cooper (George MacKay). Once a shy, boyish 20-year-old who refused to hold up a banner at a Pride march, he becomes a proud LGSM member. His sweeping character arc is articulated by the sense of belonging he feels when inside Gay's the Word. When he walks through the bookshop's door, he's safe, a feeling he has never quite been able to establish at home. There, he has a chosen family who love him not in spite of his queerness, but because of it.

"My first Pride was in '84, like Bromley, and in '85 I was on the march," MacSweeney explains. His own first time in

Gay's the Word was as a member of the Gay Icebreakers:
"They had meetings in the shops once every two weeks, I'd
go to those, and it politicised me." From rural Ireland to
bustling London, MacSweeney's own journey to the shop
informs his continued mission to foster a non-judgmental
and empathetic place. "I would have been very shy coming
into a space like this for the first time," MacSweeney goes
on. "There are times where someone's been very nervous
the first time. They come back later and they're much more
self-assured. It's really nice to see."

From the '80s to the present day, Gay's the Word has
served as a sacred location for new generations of the
LGBTQ+ community. "What I now like about the space is
how new generations have discovered us," MacSweeney
says. "Now, most of the people visiting the bookshop are
under 30. [They are] a whole new generation who want the
physicality of books and are also interested in our history.
It's not taught in schools and they want to know where the
movement comes from."

The hateful presence of homophobia does exist in *Pride*,
with distasteful attitudes towards LGSM and homophobic
graffiti on the shopfront. However, Warchus' film has
undoubtedly inspired both hopefulness and intrigue in
viewers. "What the film has done has been extraordinary
for pulling people into the shop," MacSweeney adds when I
mention *Pride*. "They see the film and they come especially.
We couldn't be more grateful. They're then aware we have
a history... I probably talk to someone about *Pride* every
day, that it's one of their favourite films or that it helped
them come out."

Pride is not the only instance of Gay's the Word being captured on film. The 1985 LGSM-made short documentary *All Out! Dancing in Dulais* also documented the South Wales miners' strike and the involvement of the LGBTQ+ community. The film is certainly less widely known and viewed. In fact, I hadn't seen the film until MacSweeney put the documentary on my radar, which captures the delicate real-life interactions that *Pride* lovingly replicates.

However, MacSweeney notes that *Pride* is not a documentary and leaves out several important details – such as the Customs and Excise raid on the bookshop in 1984, which seized all imported books, the same year LGSM joined the miners' strike. Despite these omissions, for many viewers, the film serves as an accessible and entertaining gateway to the history of the LGBTQ+ movement. As depicted in the film, Gay's the Word owners Gethin Roberts (Andrew Scott) and Jonathan Blake (Dominic West) – the second person diagnosed with HIV in the UK – cherish this bookshop as a safe space where they are truly recognised.

"Gay's the Word is a bookshop run by us for us, an undiluted living archive of queer thought and imagination," writes journalist Neil McKenna. "Like a friend who always stands by our side and encourages us on, there is a reason why the bookshop is regularly described as a haven, as a sanctuary." McKenna's sentiment is true of so many people's experiences. The bookshop isn't just a business, but a space where people are entertained, informed, and educated. It's a hub for the community that transcends any shallow facade.

Admiring the pin wall at Gay's the Word (featuring badges like "Gay Whales Against Racism") and the blue plaque honoring Mark Ashton above the shopfront serves as a powerful reminder that Gay's the Word's significance is both personal and political. It challenges the tendency of other bookshops to compartmentalize LGBTQ+ literature. "In the heteronormative world, we make adjustments to our behaviour, we police ourselves. Here, in the shop, you can let that go and just be," says MacSweeney. Instead of isolating our experience to a single bookcase, Gay's the Word makes it into an entire world. •

LGBTQ+ LONDON

01 VICTIM

1961   dir. Basil Dearden

Bogarde at his best as a closeted lawyer, risking it all to expose a blackmail ring targeting gay men in '60s London.

02 SUNDAY BLOODY SUNDAY

1971   dir. John Schlesinger

A nuanced portrayal of London's liberal elite, where queer love quietly unfolds amidst social change.

03 A BIGGER SPLASH

1973   dir. Jack Hazan

Hockney's brushstrokes bring a splash of queer love to London's art scene – and yes, it's all in the details.

04 THE NAKED CIVIL SERVANT

1975   dir. Jack Gold

Quentin Crisp takes to London's streets with defiant flair in this pioneering biopic starring the great John Hurt.

05 NIGHTHAWKS

1978   dir. Ron Peck

An unsung gem capturing London's underground gay nightlife; shot on location at real clubs for added authenticity.

06 BREAKFAST ON PLUTO

2005   dir. Neil Jordan

Cillian Murphy sensitively portrays a trans woman who flees '70s Ireland for London, looking for her birth mother.

07 DISOBEDIENCE

2017   dir. Sebastián Lelio

Forbidden love in North London's Orthodox Jewish community – Rachel Weisz and Rachel McAdams co-star.

08 BENJAMIN

2018   dir. Simon Amstell

A young, queer filmmaker's anxious quest for love unfolds in a London that feels refreshingly non-touristy.

09 REBEL DYKES

2021   dir. Harri Shanahan, Siân Williams

Punk-fueled rebellion shakes up '80s London, spotlighting a radical and defiant lesbian subculture.

10 FEMME

2023   dir. Sam H. Freeman, Ng Choon Ping

Queer identity and revenge intertwine in this gritty London thriller with Nathan Stewart-Jarrett and George MacKay.

IN *MEMORIA*

BY FEDOR TOT

Where do we choose to call home? Apichatpong Weerasethakul's transcendent mystery, screened at the BFI London Film Festival, has one writer searching for answers hate London. In a book largely celebrating the capital and its cinematic culture, that might seem like a counterintuitive way to begin – yet I've always felt the city to be a place whose organising principles are in complete opposition, philosophically and ideologically, to my own. Each time I visit, I'm reminded of Bob Hoskins' Harold Shand in *The Long Good Friday*, a cockney gangster on the precipice of a property deal that would turn London's Docklands at the birth of the '80s into the ultra-rich playground we've come to know today. The film has his character's misdeeds punished by the IRA (a youthful, pre-Bond Pierce Brosnan, no less). Offscreen, though, it ended up being the gangsters and property developers who won out – and maybe this is why every visit to the capital gnaws away at my soul, leaving me more exhausted than the time before.

I have a similarly tense relationship with the London Film Festival, which I've regularly attended, looking to bond and make connections, only to wind up feeling like a stranger in the back of an old school photo. Taking place in October each year, the LFF's programme tends to consist of a smorgasbord of the biggest films to have premiered at other major festivals, still to be released in cinemas. In theory, it's a great opportunity for audiences and industry folk to catch up on the best films of the year. In practice, I've found the LFF experience to be a lonely one, more so than at other festivals around the world. Yet year after year, I am drawn back to a city that's indifferent to me, to a festival that makes me feel like a ghost. I can't help but wonder: why?

To answer this question, let's go back to 2021. I was

standing in Soho, queue-camping with a friend in the rain, waiting for a press screening I had no idea would have a profound and transformative effect on my future relationship with cinema. Actually, I had made a promise to myself to never queue camp again, but I broke my rule for one film that year – a film that had been granted a single press screening at the Leicester Square Vue: Apichatpong Weerasethakul's *Memoria*.

It's my opinion that Weerasethakul's films are some of the few in the 21st century so far to have meaningfully pushed the art form forward. They are slow and meditative, often mixing depictions of rural life in the director's native Thailand with scenes of magical realism and surrealism. *Memoria* was his first film made outside his home country and stars Tilda Swinton as Jessica Holland, an emigrant in Bogotá, Colombia who suddenly begins to hear a booming, thudding noise at random points during the day (there is a real medical term for this, "Exploding Head Syndrome," and though generally harmless, Weerasethakul himself experienced it during his research for the film). In looking for the source of these sounds, Jessica journeys from the city to the countryside, the film shifting effortlessly between urban and rural worlds.

Despite its international setting and the starry presence of Swinton, *Memoria* is a refinement and re-focusing of Weerasethakul's primary preoccupations: the divide between urban and rural living, the ideological violence of modern capitalism, the inability of modernity to answer deeper existential questions of meaning and desire. Within Weerasethakul's contemplative, "slow cinema" aesthetics, the film explores these themes in both narrative form and stylistic structure, allowing the audience the freedom to enter something of a meditative state.

This reaches its apotheosis in a half-hour single take near the end of a film, where Jessica meets Hernán Bedoya, a villager who claims to be able to remember everything that's ever happened to him and who has never left his home village for fear of overstimulating himself. That he is the namesake of another Hernán Bedoya, a sound engineer whom Jessica meets earlier in the film and who attempts to help her find the source of the booming noise, is left tantalisingly unanswered, though the general implication seems to be that he is some sort of spiritual double, displaced across time and space (the real Hernán Bedoya was a Columbian lands rights activist, shot dead by a neo-paramilitary group in 2017 after resisting encroachment from palm oil companies).

Jessica and Hernán simply sit and converse, while Hernán guts and skins fish. The scene reaches beyond the objective reality filmed on-screen – two actors sat talking together – and infiltrates into something profound. It becomes about the ideological underpinnings of inter-human connection and empathy, even in the face of an unfriendly modern world that refuses and actively pushes against that simple connectivity. This is a film in which the space to simply *be* is given to the actors, whether major A-listers or non-professional locals. *Memoria* explores the implications of what that "simply being" means: it's a protest and a refusal to submit to the cult of productivity, hustle, and economic output that we're constantly told to embrace. In some ways, the philosophical goals of the film are at complete odds with the festival and the city in which it was programmed. Indeed, they're at odds with Cannes, where it was given its world premiere. That *Memoria* is allowed to exist in such a space feels like a welcome perversion, a recognition by someone, somewhere that cinema as art still matters.

To *be* is, for me, at least, an increasingly difficult thing. I've grown up in the UK – in Newport first, and now in Cardiff – but I've never felt at home. I have a British passport, but I consider that to be the only British thing about me, and I'm not certain about being Welsh either. I have one other passport, a Serbian one, but I don't consider myself to be Serbian. I was born in Yugoslavia, a multinational, linguistically- and religiously-mixed country, and I am from Sremski Karlovci in Vojvodina, traditionally an ethnically-mixed region, which includes Serbs, Hungarians, Germans, Roma, and plenty more. In a recent return, I've come to believe that the country has in the past few years become more hostile and negative, for reasons social and political that would take an entire book to explain. What do you do when you have two passports, but neither one is worth anything to you?

Memoria's exploration of what it means to *be* is refracted through a sense of displacement. Swinton's Jessica exists in the film as an emigrant to Columbia; what we see of her lifestyle here suggests she is reasonably well-off, as it tends to be for emigrants from the Anglosphere to Latin America. But her racial and financial privilege is also an alienatory factor in Columbia, divorcing the protagonist from the world around her. She floats through the city's spaces – traffic crossings, restaurants, and lecture halls – like a spectre. To the locals she meets, she may as well be a supernatural entity and has little to no effect on the world around her. Her journey to the countryside is met by militarized forces on the road, yet she seems to pass untouched through these spaces, too: immune she may be, but alone. The modern city often promises escape amidst anonymity for new arrivals, whether that's Bogotá or London: but that anonymity is also a trap, a kind of void in which it's very easy to disappear.

Weerasethakul's films, more broadly, nearly always deal with displacement and its causes and symptoms: historical (his Palme d'Or-winning *Uncle Boonmee Who Can Recall His Past Lives*), violent (*Cemetery of Splendour*), or sexual (*Tropical Malady*). Military forces often lurk in his films, whether it's one of the protagonists in *Tropical Malady* undertaking his military service, or the hospital filled with sleeping soldiers in *Cemetery of Splendour*. Although it's hard to recall a single outwardly violent scene in his filmography, Weerasethakul's work is tinged with the threat of violence, or of its real, physical existence in the form of militarised structures and organisations. It's this presence which often works in some way to displace the characters, divorcing their physical bodies from their souls – such as the tender gay romance that quietly blossoms in *Tropical Malady*, which is never given resolution or purpose, its very *being* in and of itself a threat. Although urban spaces are not particularly common in his films, they are linked: urban spaces are often built on violence, a long crawl of gentrification always pushing the city's poor further to the margins, and the centrality of state power flushing out to the rural periphery in the forms of armed security forces, their existence always acting on the reality of the film.

It's also this threat of violence which I think Weerasethakul's films aim to transcend – and when they achieve this feat it is precisely because they repudiate violent structures and ideologies. I sense that Weerasethakul's films reflect a sense of deeper inner peace, a kind of compromise and acceptance with a world that isn't home – a world that actively seeks to destroy, yet is one we must learn to live with... for now.

Around the release of *Memoria*, the director would often speak of the history of state violence both Columbia and Thailand share: "For Colombians, the word 'memoria' is specifically tied to the trauma and violence of the armed conflict. The title kind of shaped my approach to the film. And looking back at my research, I can see that I had unconsciously focused on this trauma already, I'd just approached it very instinctively," he said in an interview for Metrograph.

And yet, a few moments later, he jumps towards a more alchemical, intangible reading of the film's production: "In the script, there is much more this idea of the landscapes and other settings. But when I looked at Tilda, at what she contributed, it was almost like everything was embodied in her, you know? We just need her to guide us to these places. She becomes a landscape, part of the reflection, like a mirror."

That sense of inner acceptance animates my response to his films. If I'm going to make peace with the condition of permanent displacement, I also have to make peace with the sense that I can never quite *be* anywhere. *Memoria* sits in a personal canon of what one might call a cinema of displacement, films made by directors with a sense that there's not quite anywhere you can call *home*. There's a line in Pjer Žalica's *Days and Hours*, a 2004 Bosnian film dealing with grief and family history in post-war Sarajevo, in which one character says to another: "It's not important where you live, but with whom." Likewise, in the 1995 Indian film *Naseem* by Saeed Akhtar Mirza, about a Muslim family in Mumbai, the titular character asks her grandfather why the family chose to stay despite increasing hostility and violence from Hindu nationalists. "We just really loved that tree in our backyard," he says. Both statements speak to a sense of cultural and philosophical Otherness and duality. Both statements are true to anybody who has ever had to consider leaving "home," whatever that means.

Memoria forms part of that strain of thought, speaking to a broader duality of cinema, and perhaps the modern 21st-century human condition, which seems to wrap itself continually around these pointless yet all-too-real questions of ethnic and racial identity. It exists in this exploratory space in which nothing is fixed, its own dissociations and contradictions multiplying at will. The discombobulating effect of being in a city that seems hostile to my very soul found some kind of link in *Memoria*. Though the film is far from being openly antagonistic about its landscape, it's clearly a film about not being at home, about being uncomfortable and out-of-place – an exploration of what that does to one's psychogeographic headspace. It reaches out, though, in a gesture of empathy, and seeks to find some sense of solace or community in the fictions and characters it stumbles across. One of its final scenes, where Jessica and Hernán simply hold hands and look at each other across the table as an aural swirl of noise engulfs the soundspace, seems an attempt to find the source of that empathy, with two figures simply *being* alongside each other. I may have witnessed it in a somewhat anonymous multiplex screen at a festival whose identity is frankly somewhat anonymous itself – yet that rainy October day was a moment of pure and utter transportation, a reminder of cinema's capacity to blend the real and the metaphysical, a unique coalescence of space, time, and moment. And in London, of all places. Who'd have thought? •

CULTURE CLASH IN LONDON

01 ABSOLUTE BEGINNERS

1986   dir. Julien Temple

Bowie-starring musical set against '50s race riots in London. Quintessential film maudit, but plenty to love.

02 SAMMY AND ROSIE GET LAID

1987   dir. Stephen Frears

Explores a couple's open relationship against the backdrop of 1980s London's political unrest and urban decay.

03 BEAUTIFUL PEOPLE

1999   dir. Jasmin Dizdar

During a footie match in '90s London, families encounter Yugoslavian refugees at the time of the Balkan War.

04 DIRTY PRETTY THINGS

2002   dir. Stephen Frears

Ludicrous but uber-watchable heist-drama about illegal immigrants, set in a West London hotel – plenty of heart.

05 BRICK LANE

2007   dir. Sarah Gavron

In the shadow of 9/11, a young Bangladeshi girl is forcibly relocated to Brick Lane to start a new life with an older man.

06 LONDON RIVER

2009   dir. Rachid Bouchareb

Set in multicultural London after the 2005 attacks, strangers are bonded by tragedy in Harringay and Finsbury Park.

07 THE INFIDEL

2010   dir. Josh Appignanesi

A Muslim man (Omid Djalili) learns he's actually Jewish in Josh Appignanesi's London-set comedy of cultural identity.

08 MY BROTHER THE DEVIL

2012   dir. Sally El Hosaini

In gritty Hackney, this film about Egyptian siblings explores brotherhood and identity within local gang culture.

09 GONE TOO FAR!

2013   dir. Destiny Ekaragha

Peckham-set comedy explores cultural clashes and sibling dynamics among Nigerian-British teenagers.

10 THE LAST TREE

2019   dir. Shola Amoo

A Nigerian-British boy trades country life for inner-city strife; amidst the high-rises of South London, he struggles to assimilate.

LOVE AND CONCRETE

BY LILIA PAVIN-FRANKS

The city's brutalism so often serves as the face of dystopia and disintegration. Yet, within these spaces, feelings of romance manage to break through

A t the joyous climax of Peckham-set romcom *Rye Lane*, the film's leads finally profess their love for one another after almost ninety minutes of will-they-won't-they antics. Dom (David Jonsson) stands inside an artsy glass tower block, looking out toward Yas (Vivian Oparah), who waves ecstatically from a boat as it sails down the Thames. As the pair race to meet, we're given a tour of their surroundings: the Tate Modern, the Millennium Bridge, the industrial buildings lining the bankside. The camera pans 360 degrees around the pair to capture their first kiss, as London's stony Southbank architecture watches on, benevolent and hazy in a soft-focus glow.

It's a moment that reaffirms what I've always found to be true: there's something romantic about concrete. Though I've never experienced a grand declaration of love akin to that in *Rye Lane* (yet!), the area just south of the river holds a special place in my heart, providing a home to not only my job at the UK's centre of cinema, the British Film Institute, but also dance, theatre, music, and fine art in the brutalist complex incorporating the National Theatre and the Royal Festival Hall. Within these grey, labyrinthine structures, amid the dense population of artsy types browsing the stalls of local booksellers or the array of busking performers, you'd be hard-pressed to resist the stirring romance of creativity coming from every direction.

Asked to consider London's great on-screen love stories, you might first think of the bright bouquets and charming bookshops found on Portobello Road. But between brutalist buildings and pebbledash walls lie some of the warmest and most intimate relationships in film, in works that often delve deeper into the complexities of love than those starring floppy-haired Hugh Grants and Colin Firths – narratives interwoven with themes of queerness, race, and class that better understand London as it exists in real life.

Post-war modernist and brutalist structures prioritised function over beauty and utilised versatile and cheap materials like concrete in the interest of saving time and money after the Second World War. Often built for public housing, these council estates were regarded as unappealing and overbearing grey structures, associated with unwanted social unrest harbouring fear, crime, and isolation. But, in all its inherent rigidity, concrete in film has proven more pliable when it comes to adding contours to romance; the unyielding banality of the material juxtaposing the tenderness of the love within. Maybe it's the aesthetic conformity of these spaces that allows characters' self-actualisation to feel so much more vibrant and meaningful – the transient nature of the self in contrast with the immovability of the concrete form.

Scenes set on concrete rooftops in both 1991's *Young Soul Rebels* and 2012's *Stud Life* are crucial to emotional breakthroughs. The former, Isaac Julien's searing thriller about the social landscape of 1970s Britain, and national, racial, and queer identity, may not spring to mind immediately when thinking about pure romance, but there's undeniable heart nestled within its socio-political commentary. After conflicts about their respective love interests and different priorities about their DJ careers, best friends Caz and Chris (Mo Sesay and Valentine Nonyela) come to a head up high, emotions finally boiling over. Climbing to the rooftop to interfere with the signals and get their pirate radio station out to larger audiences, a close-up shot focuses on their hands, intimately overlapping, as they tape their radio transmitter onto the aerial. Chris slips and almost falls, but Caz grabs his arm, rescuing him. In an instant, the emotional intensity between the two shifts in tone, and an argument ensues. Though they disagree with the other's priorities, the anger of both men comes from a place of love and commitment, arms snaking round bodies, faces intimately close as they shout about loyalty. "I thought I was supposed to be your main man," Caz cries. "What are you talking about?" Chris responds. "You *are* my main man!"

This physical and emotional intimacy – an exposed tower block rooftop as a setting for roiling emotion – is also utilised in Campbell X's queer romance *Stud Life*, which sees wedding photographer JJ (T'Nia Miller) balance love, friendship and gender identity in London. She and girlfriend Elle (Robyn Kerr) share a kiss on a rooftop, the orange hue of the setting sun bathing them in a warm, seductive light. A skyscraper can be seen in the distance, glowering above the sharp, jagged cityscape – looming, yet unthreatening. This often vilified space provides a sanctum for the two to revel in soft touches and sweet kisses, at once exposed but also cradled as they tower over the masses on the sultry, sun-drenched rooftop without being seen from below. As they move indoors, JJ begins to express her emotions to Elle – her complex and layered feelings about sex and gender mirroring the multi-layered spaces she and her friends inhabit. Campbell X subverts stereotypes of high-density housing through heady and warm cinematography: *Stud Life* doesn't make concrete feel dangerous or isolating, but passionate and safe.

Likewise, in Hettie MacDonald's vibrant 1996 rom-com *Beautiful Thing*, primary colours are used in abundance to offset the grey of the concrete block of council flats. The film revolves around bullied teen Jamie (Glen Barry) and his coming to terms with his queerness and love for neighbour Ste (Scott Neal) in 90s London – specifically London's Thamesmead estate, most famously used in Stanley Kubrick's *A Clockwork Orange* as the violent playground for his scuzzy "droogs." Here, front doors are painted blue, the boys wear bright red football shirts, Jamie and mum Sandra's home boasts sunshine yellow walls and hanging baskets brim with red flowers. These infusions of colour bring the estate to life and mirror the eclecticism of its inhabitants – and are also a far cry from the dystopian nightmare Kubrick created on the very same set.

Centring on the power of a different kind of love, Charlotte Regan's 2023 *Scrapper* – a sweet tale of a father and daughter's newfound relationship in the wake of loss – takes the perspective of its kid protagonist, Georgie (Lola Campbell), and aesthetically mirrors her juvenile outlook on life. Looking as if the camera has been doused in a child's dream of glitter and sugary sprinkles, *Scrapper* juxtaposes the kitchen-sink realism of council estate-set films with magical realism (producer Theo Barrowclough explained that they weren't setting out to make a Ken Loach film). As viewers, we're constantly invited to see things as Georgie sees them in her zany imagination; in the same vein as *Beautiful Thing*, *Scrapper* also rejects the cold, grey image of a council estate by splattering the homes in pastel colours, with Georgie's in particular decorated with a joyous and hopeful shade of yellow. In the film's closing scene, the protagonists paint the house themselves, creating a defiant visual rejection of this stereotyped space.

There's an abundance of graffiti in 2023's *Rye Lane*, too. The areas Dom and Yas move through – namely, the streets of Peckham – are often concrete-clad and covered in graffiti, but *Rye Lane* romanticises Peckham and its outbursts of creativity in the same way Richard Curtis does in *Notting Hill* – full of vibrancy, emotion, and potential. A subtle fish-eye lens warps the solid lines of the architecture, feeding the space into the bodies of the characters so that the distinction between the two seems to melt away. Low-angled shots emphasise how Dom and Yas exist within certain spaces, as huge, solid buildings tower around them protectively.

Perhaps the most effusive display of concrete's innate romanticism, though, comes in the closing scene of *Beautiful Thing*. In a moment of tenderness and joy, Ste and Jamie – both newly comfortable in their love and their queerness – share an intimate dance on the grounds of the Thamesmead estate. Embraced in each other's arms, they sway as the non-diegetic soundtrack croons "Dream a Little Dream of Me" by The Mamas & the Papas. With Ste and Jamie at the centre, the camera tracks around them, the high rise of concrete blocks present in the background, the pair made golden in the evening sun – much like the aforementioned climax of *Rye Lane*. A small crowd gathers around, looking on at the dancing with fondness. The diverse crowd grows larger, people of all ages and races happily swaying to the music. The scene is a direct aesthetic and narrative rejection of the story that's often written about these people, but never by them.

Historically, concrete buildings and public housing have been tainted as liminal and antisocial spaces – particularly in cities like London – in no small part due to the raw melancholy favoured by filmmakers like Ken Loach and Andrea Arnold. But cinema can also show us their true romantic potential, uncovering the very real intimacies residing within. And yes, *Notting Hill* and *Bridget Jones's Diary* will likely prevail as the most beloved cinematic representations of the city – I admit, I will always relate to the eponymous blonde, lovelorn woman – but the wealth of films outside the canon also deserve just as much credit for cementing London as a city of love. •

BRUTALIST LONDON

01 THE LONG ARM

1956   dir. Charles Frend

Compelling London police noir starring Jack Hawkins, with a climactic shot at Southbank's Royal Festival Hall.

02 FAHRENHEIT 451

1966   dir. François Truffaut

Truffaut travelled to Roehampton in his '60s adaptation of the classic novel, shooting at the sprawling Alton Estate.

03 A CLOCKWORK ORANGE

1971   dir. Stanley Kubrick

Violent gangs roam Kubrick's Brutalist vision of London, famously filmed in Thamesmead and Wandsworth.

04 THE PASSENGER

1975   dir. Michelangelo Antonioni

Jack Nicholson's journo on the run briefly decamps to London, where he drops by Bloomsbury's Brunswick Centre.

05 THE MEDUSA TOUCH

1978   dir. Jack Gold

A plane crashes into the top of London's Centre Point skyscraper in this psychokinetic horror with Richard Burton.

06 THE HUNGER

1983   dir. Tony Scott

Eerie vampire vibes from Scott, actually set in New York. But the ending features an all-time great shot of a Barbican Estate high-rise.

07 FOR QUEEN AND COUNTRY

1988   dir. Martin Stellman

Denzel Washington crosses the pond to play a British paratrooper; solid anti-Thatcher thrills, featuring the Trellick Tower.

08 SHOPPING

1994   dir. Paul W. S. Anderson

This dystopian heist flick from Paul W. S. Anderson plays out in the shadows of brutalist gems like the Trellick Tower.

09 GANGSTER NO. 1

2000   dir. Paul McGuigan

Thewlis' thug lives in Shakespeare Tower, Barbican in this timeline-hopping gangster flick from Paul McGuigan.

10 BREAKING AND ENTERING

2006   dir. Anthony Minghella

Class warfare from Minghella – his last effort before his untimely death, North London-set and starring Jude Law.

THE GREEN ZONE

BY RAFA SALES ROSS

Alfonso Cuarón's chilling depiction of future London offered a prescient look at what could be – or what now is. But is there a message of hope at the heart of *Children of Men*?

n the two centuries since its establishment following the British naval victory in the Napoleonic Wars, Trafalgar Square has become one of London's most distinctive landmarks. Walking from Leicester Square into the vast courtyard is something of a sightseer's treat: pass the dizzying lights and signs of West End theatres, turn a corner by the neatly concealed entrance to the National Portrait Gallery, and there you are, standing amongst floods of pigeons and excited tourists. Look to the right and you'll see the Pantheon-inspired National Gallery; to the left, the peeking crown of Big Ben, nested atop the Houses of Parliament.

Many films have captured Trafalgar Square in all its cinematic glory, from clever Dalmatian Pongo dragging Roger Dearly (Jeff Daniels) to meet his beloved Anita (Joely Richardson) in Stephen Herek's 1996 live-action adaptation of *101 Dalmatians*, to David Kessler dramatically crossing the square on his way to an altruistic confession in John Landis' 1981 cult classic *An American Werewolf in London*. Superheroes from Wonder Woman to Captain America have passed through the infamous piazza, and so have several generations of the most infamous agent in the British Secret Service, including a meeting between Daniel Craig's recent iteration and quartermaster Q (Ben Whishaw) by a Turner painting in the National Gallery in 2012's *Skyfall*.

The same iconic spot features in Alfonso Cuarón's 2006 dystopia *Children of Men*, but instead of Dalmatians plotting to make two people fall in love or MI6 spies confronting cartoonish villains, the film showcases the square as an unsafe, rowdy epicentre of unrest. This is because Cuarón's prescient thriller takes place in the near future, in 2027, when women have lost their ability to bear children and so the world has gone to hell.

Adapted from P.D. James' 1992 novel *The Children of Men*, the film is set in England on the brink of extinction, where societal collapse has amplified the country's historical penchant for authoritarianism, Britain now a tyrannical state where immigrants are segregated into modern concentration camps and terrorist bombings have become so common that not even limbs violently catapulted into the air can disturb one's morning coffee. Decades on, Cuarón's dystopia has seeped into the edges of the present day, a snapshot of London that plays not as a cautionary tale but as a gruelling encompassment of Britain's current sociopolitical unravelling.

It is in the minutes that precede the aforementioned bombing that we first meet Theo Faron (Clive Owen). The scruffy civil servant impatiently squeezes his way into a small crowd that gathers under an old television in a coffee shop where stale pastries sit unwanted and watery espressos are handed over by the dozen. The newscast has everyone in a state of shared shock – the youngest person in the world, 18-year-old "Baby Diego," has been stabbed to death in his home country of Argentina during a pub brawl. With one swift piercing of a knife, the world has gotten a little older, hope sliding further and further away.

The curious thing is, if Baby Diego were to make his way from Argentina to England where mourners grieve his death, he'd be imprisoned alongside thousands of others. The towering buildings of Fleet Street, where the coffee shop sits, are mere meters away from Tube stations where ticket barriers stand next to massive cages filled to the brim with human beings. Thanks to the safety of its geography, you see, England has become one of the few countries still able to maintain some form of order in this near future when the world grows increasingly unstable. Such a sense of security has millions flocking to British shores in search of a better future, an illusion promptly destroyed upon arrival. As people scream for help, one can almost hear former Home Secretary Suella Braverman's words echoing around the wasteland: "It's not racist for anyone, ethnic minority or otherwise, to want to control our borders."

"The world has collapsed – only Britain soldiers on," blares a screen inside the heavily secured bus that takes Theo home from work following a pantomime performance of grief that convinces his boss to give him half a day off. The commercials are seen not only on the small screens inside public transport but in massive billboards suspended above crumbling Halifax branches and decrepit megastores. When the past comes knocking on Theo's door, it does so in the shape of a sleazy van with its windows concealed with a collage of newspapers that tell a brief history of the time: "Armageddon begins: Russia detonates nuclear bomb, Kazakhstan annihilated"; "Test tube Daisy dies"; "Chaos in refugee camps"; "Protest against government's new racist policies."

"We cannot allow one single frame of this film to go without a comment on the state of things," said *Children of Men* cinematographer and Cuarón's long-standing creative partner Emmanuel Lubezki, reflecting on the film's sense of visual storytelling. It was through a refined marriage of cinematography and production design that the Mexican director found a way to cleverly bypass the overexposition that often follows sci-fi films – the reality of the year 2027 is told here through newspapers plastered on old vans, graffiti on crumbling walls, the ever-present chatter coming from slick TV screens.

In *Children of Men*, London itself is text, its familiar landscape expanding as a book to tell a story of future despair that unravels not as a hyperbolic fantasy but through the terrifying hum of reality. In the years that followed the film's original release, Cuarón has been steadfast in negating any statements that portrayed him as a prophet – the signs were there (with an almost blinding clarity) to those willing to see. Using London as a central location to this sharp dissection of migration, climate change, and rampant authoritarianism not only taps into this notion of familiarity to ground *Children of Men* in attentive prescience but actively harnesses it to demonstrate the fragility of this ecosystem many believe may be able to prevent societal collapse. And, while London only serves as the background for the film's first act, its use as to embody the rotten sociopolitical values that have led modern civilization to an end is so deeply effective the city becomes synonym with the idea of *Children of Men* – a bleak ghost of failed multiculturalism haunting the edges of eerie – and presumably empty – Victorian buildings.

Speaking to *FILMdetail* upon the film's DVD release in 2007, Cuarón mentioned how reality and fiction dangerously overlapped during the shooting of the film in

2005. The coffee shop scene was shot mere days after the 7/7 bombings, a series of coordinated suicide attacks carried out by terrorists on London's public transport. "The scary thing was that a lot of the stuff that we were predicting was going to happen 10 years on started happening immediately," he explained. Many other occurrences within the film would prove eerily farsighted, with *Children of Men* returning to the public discourse at every point of cataclysmic societal change, be it Brexit in 2016, the COVID-19 pandemic in 2020, or the ongoing migration crisis in Europe.

Children of Men, much like Cuarón's seminal 2001 road movie *Y tu mama también*, is a film about impermanence, told through constant movement. This only makes it more impressive to think of how impactful its portrayal of London is. The Admiralty Arch is employed as a physical marker of the division between the wealthy and the poor. The centuries-old structure welcomes Theo into the alternative reality of The Mall, the strip of land between Marlborough and the Horse Guards that, in the year 2027, is available only to those with the deepest pockets. From the historical curves of the Arch to the modern lines of the Millennium Bridge, it turns out that one of the most classically futuristic designs can be seen in Cuarón's purposefully non-futuristic vision. The modern runway takes the greenery of one of London's few remaining parks to the imposing façade of the fictional Ark of Arts, which takes its exterior from the Battersea Power Station and its interior from the Tate Modern.

The Ark of Arts is biblical only in name. Inside its austere walls, greed lingers amongst works that have inspired – and defined – many generations of artists and thinkers. A Pink Floyd inflatable pig floats above the mirroring towers of the Battersea Power Station as Theo looks outside the window of his cousin Nigel's (Danny Huston) apartment, where he works as an overseer. Banksy's *Kissing Coppers* is guarded by government security at the entrance of the building and two large dogs sleep quietly by the feet of Michelangelo's David, displayed in the flat's lavish entry hallway. Nigel and Theo dine like kings in front of Picasso's *Guernica*, the famed painter's response to the bombing of the eponymous Basque Country town during the Spanish Civil War, as Nigel's emotionally frigid son frolics with a nondescript gadget, not glancing at the art – or the people around him – even once.

Here, art has become mere window dressing. History, despite its physical presence, has lost meaning in a world where reality is thwarted by the minute, society far too concerned with the future to harbour any preoccupations about the past. This is symbolised by the hoards of Repenters occupying Trafalgar Square, who kneel down for an entire month in the hopes of salvation and chant in unison to catechise others and strengthen their cause. "The faithless have made us barren," say the signs lifted above their heads, the same God that once led England's naval ships to glory in infamous battles like Trafalgar now blamed for the annihilation of mankind.

By the time *Children of Men* came to fruition, Cuarón was no stranger to putting a dark twist on beloved British institutions, having helmed an instalment of the Harry Potter franchise, 2004's *Harry Potter and the Prisoner of*

Azkaban. For me, a young Brazilian girl whose perception of London was guided solely by teenage wizards, *Children of Men* introduced a grittier alternative – a world that eschewed the magical in favour of a darker, more sinister London, where danger lurked in centuries-old alleyways. It felt like a friendly warning, a token of Latin camaraderie. The London of *Akzaban* and, subsequently, the London of *Children of Men*, felt tangible, closer to home. It dissolved the idea of the perfect land of proper politeness so often propagated by colonisers to the colonised.

To peg Cuarón's unique interpretation of London solely on his foreign viewpoint would be a simplistic summary of the director's sharp eye for storytelling and world creation. But there is something to be said of seeing the English capital through the eyes of a Mexican director who has previously claimed to have set out to portray London after his home country in *Children of Men* – "to bring the third world into London" – and to see London as a city that, despite its grittiness and unrest, is still capable of inspiring a desire for change and rebirth.

In a lengthy *Vulture* interview conducted to celebrate the film's 10th anniversary, Cuarón mentioned the idea of "a green zone" – the name given to the heavily fortified 4-square-mile patch of land in the capital of Iraq described by *The Atlantic* in 2004 as "the American bubble in Baghdad" – while thinking of London as the location for *Children of Men*. "You see this Mexico. *[He moves his arm to gesture at the rest of the restaurant].* Look around and see all these beautiful people drinking their cocktails. Man, we can go ten minutes away and you go to the absolutely other extreme. But we live in these green zones that are protected. Ultimately, the U.K. looks like a green zone for the world."

Such a rationale would have easily eluded someone born and raised within the generous bosom of Eurocentrism, but it is one that greatly enhances Cuarón's future classic, which might initially feel like a parsimonious portrayal of London but eventually reveals itself to be rooted in hope – even if the sentiment first presents itself as elusively as the city's labyrinthine cobbled streets.

For as long as London stands for the bloodshed of imperialism, it also stands as a reminder of the beautiful hues of multiculturalism. A city unravelling as a patchwork of languages, peoples, and possibilities.

May it always be reborn as a miracle, from the barren womb of hatred. •

LONDON AT THE END OF THE WORLD

01 THE DAY THE EARTH CAUGHT FIRE

1961   dir. Val Guest

As London swelters under a global heatwave, a press reporter races against time to uncover the truth.

02 NINETEEN EIGHTY-FOUR

1984   dir. Michael Radford

Orwell's classic makes for bleak, oppressive viewing thanks to Radford's meticulous production design.

03 LIFEFORCE

1985   dir. Tobe Hooper

The only horror movie to feature Brent Cross Shopping Centre? Vamps swarm London in this so-bad-it's good gem.

04 28 DAYS LATER...

2002   dir. Danny Boyle

The quality of the DV footage is as scary as the fast zombies who populate this film's vision of infected London.

05 SHAUN OF THE DEAD

2004   dir. Edgar Wright

What if the zombie apocalypse went down in... Crouch End? Still hilarious slice of comedy fried gold.

06 V FOR VENDETTA

2005   dir. James McTeigue

A fascist dictator looms large over this vision of 2020 London, a reworked Orwellian nightmare of anarchists and insurgents.

07 CHILDREN OF MEN

2006   dir. Alfonso Cuarón

Cuarón's gritty London vision is both striking and familiar: dystopian viewing that feels like it could happen tomorrow.

08 ATTACK THE BLOCK

2011   dir. Joe Cornish

John Boyega defends South London against an alien invasion in this comedy sci-fi; filmed on the former Heygate Estate.

09 HIGH-RISE

2015   dir. Ben Wheatley

J.G. Ballard's classic novel by way of Ben Wheatley, in which residents of a dystopian tower block drive themselves mad.

10 THE KITCHEN

2023   dir. Daniel Kaluuya, Kibwe Tavares

The Kitchen is a favela-like housing estate in near future London, setting of this gripping class warfare thriller.

MIKE & ME

BY ANNA MCKIBBIN

Mike Leigh is one of cinema's most prolific chroniclers of London life – his body of work asks us to consider our place in the messiness of city living, for better or worse 'd been to London before, of course, though my first definitive memory of the city came during my first week at university, as I embarked on a suitably intimidating – and then underwhelming – Freshers' Week. The student union had organised a double-decker bus (good, cool) to take a group of awkwardly dressed 18-year-olds to the infamous Ministry of Sound (bad, deeply uncool). I remember the bus as it turned a corner, a sea of heads craning around to see the twinkling outline of the cityscape from Tower Bridge.

It's a view I've encountered countless times since that moment, though one that has only reduced in clarity, coloured by a shade of tackiness and an edge of urgency as my calendar has only grown busier, the skyline now appearing as a mere scribble in the margins of the everyday. But over time the same image, seared into my subconscious, has clarified into an ideal. It is representative of newness and potential, indicative of the ill-informed notions that brought me to London in the first place. A memory of a memory; barely there and yet the only tangible proof of the city as I once imagined it.

Like me, director Mike Leigh moved to London for university, intent on studying acting before blistering against the limits of performance. Leigh's experience of London and of cinema are fundamentally connected, forever welded together, the pinpoint in timelines overlapping. Over a period, as a filmmaker, he whittled down a directorial language that exists somewhere on the razor's edge between slow-burn cinéma vérité and Greek mythology. He deconstructs the peculiar passions that hide beneath the veneer of faux politeness, exposing each bloody and bruised organ of English life with surgical skill. His mentors were not physically present, instead dispensing wisdom from the picturehouse near his student flat on Tottenham Court Road. For Leigh, it was Yasujirō Ozu and Miloš Forman; for me, it was Leigh.

Leigh's films are famous for their unnerving realism, exposing the same exhaustion of growing up and into a place that I, too, have felt since first moving to London. His characters stumble through the streets with a carefully choreographed recklessness, lurching into supposed self-actualisation before retreating when they are burned. Each plot is harsh and unsparing, exploring how circumstances can splinter and constrict into unliveable shapes. And yet these characters are never without connections – nets that keep them tangled in the web of life even when they would rather fall through. In the process, Leigh has carved out a strangely optimistic niche, a politically charged space which expressly condemns the rigours of class to make room for people's grand, irrepressible multiplicity.

Due to his pragmatic, unusual style of filmmaking (where actors rehearse for months in advance, writing the script as the plot reveals itself to them), Leigh's films are not marked by a consistent visual theme. Instead, these stories map onto the existing topography, more often than not using London's web of alleys, roads, and suburbs to make sense of the ensuing journeys of the films' characters.

Filmmakers like Leigh have earned a somewhat religious standing in the world, reorienting real lives through stories. In retrospect, it is clear that I would inevitably be drawn to directors with this degree of gravitas – those who could quietly nudge the world off its axis with each new offering. Growing up, film and religion were positioned in dizzying proximity to one another, often scheduled side by side. After church every Sunday, my parents would take my brother and I to one of Manila's chain DVD stores, and every Tuesday night while my parents were in their Bible study, the kids would be sequestered in a side room to watch a film, oscillating between family-friendly classics (*The Princess Bride*) and movies that have been rightly swallowed by history, only to be remembered by this small group of exasperated missionary kids (*Baby's Day Out*). They were two sides to the same obsessive coin, the most consistent voices in my life, tug-of-warring for my attention. As I fell deeper into an obsessive love of film, the requirements of my Christianity grew more stringent, worldly passions warned off as false idols. By the time I moved back to Northern Ireland in 2014, I was a pretty confused teenager who had grown up believing that a lot of the art I loved was compromising the religion I grew up in.

London felt like the key to these conflicting desires, a city that seemed bound by mystically artistic impulses, where I would be able to ignore the religiously motivated expectations I had struggled against. It felt like a cruel trick when I realised that the ephemeral image I had carved dissolved under the weight of an actual life. Like religion – like everything – London and art are made meaningful by the people who are there. When I left my last church, it was in a series of stuttering leaps, a gradual slinking away from my responsibilities as a member. Movies did very little to ease the guilt of leaving those relationships to decompose. Any attempt to run from the rigours of community towards the idea of emancipation, of clarity, would just end in disappointment.

Happy-Go-Lucky is one of Leigh's great London-based works. On its surface, it is a story that could be dismissed as un-cinematic, forgoing any obvious progression and following the impenetrably positive primary school teacher Poppy (Sally Hawkins) as she tries to make it through the day. More so than perhaps any of Leigh's other characters, though, she is thrilled with her life, thriving in the experience of transforming difficult things into meaningful ones. There is a shot towards the end of the film that has woven its way into my aspirations. Poppy stands on Tim's (Samuel Roukin) balcony after a successful first date. She is clad in an oversized T-shirt, her bare legs crossed playfully as she leans on the metal railing. London is spread out beneath her, as though she is balanced on one of the distant, glittering skyscrapers. It is a moment blanketed in a heady peace, one earned through the vulnerability of knowing and being known – even briefly.

When I was in my final year of university, two friends and I moved into a flat on the 24th floor of an East London high-rise. Our balcony looked out over the crystallised lights of a sparkling and sanitised Canary Wharf. That year would mark a final attempt to fit in at my legalistic student church, which collapsed into an inevitable, religion-induced nervous breakdown. There were countless mornings and evenings spent on the balcony's fold-out chairs, all sense of communication frozen solid as I grew less capable of expressing the futility of my place in the world. The contours of my existential dread were difficult to feel out, but the results were a few months of unbearably anxious Sundays where I felt the full weight of other churchgoers' judgement.

Since then, I have grown only more endeared to *Happy-Go-Lucky's* image of well-earned serenity, self-surrendered to a web of connection with no fear of the outcome. Poppy's existence, her job, her gaggle of loyal friends, are indicative of a small life worth living. In an early scene, this group drifts from Poppy's flat after a night out, and the camera catches them in a wide balcony shot from the living room window upstairs, framing early morning London as quiet, wide, and generous with potential. This has become a guiding light, the intangible argument that pulled me from organised religion and striving towards something more disparate, less hierarchal.

Leigh responds to the overwhelming, expanding size of London by focusing in on a small group of people, only occasionally stepping back to remind the audience of how connected (willingly or otherwise) they are to one another. It is an approach both boldly unsentimental and earth-shatteringly simple. *Happy-Go-Lucky* doesn't mark a shift in Leigh's filmography so much as it offers an accessible viewpoint to understand his relationship with this city as a filmmaker. It is a place packed with side alleys and wide, open roads, a place where you can elatedly ride your bike across the River Thames and have it stolen later the same day (both of which happen in the film's first 10 minutes).

The aforementioned balcony shot acts as the idealistic endpoint to all of Leigh's films, the hopeful conclusion to a career that has almost stumbled into its particular humanism. His work, perhaps unintentionally, argues that our salvation lies in one another, even if, at the same time, our relationships also trap us, reinforcing our anxieties and fears. When I first started working through his filmography, I did so in a kind of mangled reverse order. As I moved back to his start in filmmaking, I was deeply moved by the discovery that his films are rooted in this consistent kind of interpersonal potential, always conveyed through the relationship between looking and space.

High Hopes, Leigh's third theatrically-released feature film, ends with a similar shot of his newly reinvigorated characters looking out across London, scrambling to start the day. Following a group of people desperate to wrestle their lives into shapes that resemble the ideals they uphold, *High Hopes* is a comedy about people's worldviews colliding in increasingly disastrous ways. In the end, Shirley (Ruth Sheen) and Cyril (Phil Davis) have taken in Cyril's curmudgeonly mother (Edna Doré), whose veneer of stoicism has cracked to reveal someone starved of connection. Before this, *High Hopes* had been confined to the cramped confines of London flats – a web of tense confrontations amplified by the city's constant lack of space, an endless stretch of terraced houses where the walls seem to close in and the ceilings rise ever higher.

Two years later, *Life Is Sweet* would be released, cementing Leigh as one of the great chroniclers of the British working class. The film draws to a close with a similar wide shot of a North London suburb, ushered in by a more intimate conversation between two sisters sitting in front of a ramshackle shed. Natalie (Claire Skinner) and Nicola (Jane Horrocks) have spent the bulk of the film squabbling over petty matters, but in the end they are left to sift through the rubble of their fights. Natalie admits to hearing Nicola's vomiting through the night: "I think we should do something about it... you and me." In the end, the thin bedroom walls can't contain the springs of frustration. All this hurt will flow into the same, shared well. No one's fears dissipate, but in expressing them, the load is evened out. Their lives may not be what they want them to be, but they are far easier to live when enacted alongside one another.

Midway through *High Hopes*, Cyril and Shirley find themselves standing in front of Karl Marx's Tomb in Highgate Cemetery. After a few silent moments, cocooned by the trees overhead, Cyril reads the inscription on the grave: "philosophers have only interpreted the world in various ways; the point is to change it." It is a line of thinking which covertly guides Leigh's entire body of work, which is positioned in favour of people. With each of his films, he slinks further away from the ideal of the city, embracing the messy physicality of the human beings within. Just like my first memory of Tower Bridge gave way to something richer, fuller, and more demanding, Leigh's London is worth living in *because* it is a messy place. The cracks in London's façade have been there from the very beginning, and Leigh's mission has always been to shatter the illusion and sit amongst the shards. •

MIKE LEIGH'S LONDON

01 MEANTIME

1983   dir. Mike Leigh

Working-class struggles in Thatcherite Britain? Leigh's bread and butter. This Gary Oldman-starring TV film is a doozy.

02 HIGH HOPES

1988   dir. Mike Leigh

King's Cross-set class comedy (but sad!) about an optimistic couple, their snobby neighbours, and associates.

03 NAKED

1993   dir. Mike Leigh

A brilliant but broken Northerner (David Thewlis) descends on London and brings himself to ruin. Dalston-centric.

04 SECRETS & LIES

1996   dir. Mike Leigh

Leigh's crowning achievement? Stunningly humane drama about a Black woman seeking her birth mother in East London.

05 CAREER GIRLS

1997   dir. Mike Leigh

Two estranged friends reunite in a cramped London flat. Look out for Andy Serkis as a terrible estate agent.

06 TOPSY-TURVY

1999   dir. Mike Leigh

Leigh goes full Victorian with this joyous, highly original exploration of theatre legends Gilbert and Sullivan.

07 ALL OR NOTHING

2002   dir. Mike Leigh

Timothy Spall and Leslie Manville are a couple in crisis in this sadly comic drama, set on a London housing estate.

08 VERA DRAKE

2004   dir. Mike Leigh

Portrait of a woman who performs illegal abortions in '50s London; it bagged the Golden Lion at Venice.

09 HAPPY-GO-LUCKY

2008   dir. Mike Leigh

Teacher Poppy is joy incarnate, taking whatever the city throws at her (crazed cab drivers, bike thieves) in her stride.

10 ANOTHER YEAR

2010   dir. Mike Leigh

Four seasons spent in the company of an ageing East London couple; Leigh at his mercurial best – wise, witty, sad, true.

TUNNEL VISIONS

BY YASMIN OMAR

Permissions. Permits. A heck of a lot of patience. What does it really take to film a scene on the London Underground?

The first time I really felt like a Londoner was when I became familiar with the Tube – when I could decipher its clean, colour-coded lines and advise helpless tourists on their journeys through its labyrinthine network. Passing through the Underground, I was a cartographer mapping out my own sentimental topography of the city. Soon, stations were memories, rather than just place names. Tottenham Hale was where I had participated in an impromptu, whole-carriage singalong of "Love on Top" on the way back from a Beyoncé concert. Finchley Road was where I had witnessed a very intoxicated woman throw up Barney-purple sick on her shoes at the puzzlingly early hour of 6pm. The Tube is London's central nervous system, ferrying us around and triggering all manner of emotional responses.

In a nod to the "romanticise your life" trend that promotes finding joy in the mundane, the comedian Catherine Cohen considers certain everyday behaviours as "lady in a movie" activities, like holding a baguette or unlocking a post box. Riding the London Underground – where you could meet anyone, be anyone – also fits the bill. The Tube has certainly been in a *lot* of movies over the years: there's the Alfred Hitchcock cameo as a disgruntled commuter in his first talkie *Blackmail*, the Tottenham Court Road chase sequence in *An American Werewolf in London*, the heartwarming Maida Vale montage in the romantic comedy *About Time*....

The demand to shoot on the Underground became so high that, since 1992, Transport for London has employed Kate Reston as its film office manager. A movie-lover with a 12-foot cinema screen at home, she, along with her team, oversees every stage of the planning and execution process. "American projects, particularly, will have a telephone box, a black taxi, and an Underground logo to establish London," she says. "Nothing speaks to London more than the Underground roundel."

So how does it happen? To film on the Tube, the first thing a production needs is a permit. To acquire one, they must send their screenplay to the TfL Film Office, who receive "at least 500" applications a year. "One of the most important things is that we like to be seen in at least a neutral light and not a negative one," Reston explains. "We're always flexible. We'll look at scripts and say you need to tweak this a bit. Some people work with it, some people won't. There's a limit to what you can do. It's not Thomas the Tank Engine, you can't pick up trains and put them wherever you like." Requests also need to comply with TfL regulations – which prohibit depictions of smoking, vandalism, and fare evasion, among other frowned upon activities. "Top of the list of asks, unfortunately, tends to be terrorism, which we're not keen to show. I always say, 'Give me one airline that's ever put their name to something where there's a disaster.'" Once everything has been agreed, and the necessary rewrites are made, the TfL personnel involved will sign an NDA, which Reston reckons is "fair enough," since "they've paid a considerable fee to be there."

The fees are indeed steep. Filming in an operational station costs from £900 an hour, and using an "exclusive area" closed to the public (i.e. disused stations such as Aldwych, which shut in 1994, or the Jubilee Line at Charing

Cross, which put an end to service in 1999) costs from £2,000 an hour. Rest assured that the funds collected are reinvested back into the transport network, and the film office's revenue has grown each year. The popularity of Tube stations as filming locations ebbs and flows over time. When Reston initially took on the position, shoots predominantly took place in East Finchley, which rarely sees action these days. Now, the most sought-after stations are Bank and Aldwych – both exclusive areas, allowing for greater availability and control – and Canary Wharf. "People still want the typical olde worlde Underground, but we're always looking for other locations," says Reston. "We recently checked out the old tunnels at Shepherd's Bush. It would be nice to use the Elizabeth Line, too. We had more enquiries while it was still under construction than we did after it was over."

The three key practical considerations Reston thinks about are: crew size, equipment load, and access times. Based on this information, she can recommend an appropriate station. "We definitely gear bigger crews towards an exclusive site because it makes it much easier for them, and it's certainly easier for us," she says. "First and foremost, we're a transport service. We have to fit in around that, not the other way around." For this reason, they restrict crew numbers in Zones One and Two, and never allow operational stations to be used during rush hour. The next step is a filmmaker recce. After a safety briefing, the relevant production members will head down to the station, take pictures, and see if it fits their brief. "Directors have a vision in their head of what they're looking for. Lots of features visit, but they may or may not come to anything. *Mission: Impossible* does the rounds a lot, they like to look at so many locations – actually one of my first projects at TfL was working on the Liverpool Street safehouse for the first film. I've got a photograph of Tom Cruise coming out of it somewhere."

Station secured, the production's art director works out how to dress it to suit the film's needs, be that transforming Canary Wharf into a spaceship for *Rogue One: A Star Wars Story* or Aldwych into a World War II bomb shelter for *Atonement*. This work is carried out under TfL guidance. "They submit their plans and we ask for specifications," Reston tells me. "The advertising also needs to be removed, and they have to put up their own for clearance purposes. We will look at their posters and check that they meet our guidelines." Often, stations will stand in for each other so that they fit geographically in a film's narrative – *Atonement*, for instance, uses Aldwych as a substitute for Balham – meaning that signage is updated in accordance with the transport network's intellectual property.

Then come the shoot days themselves, which Reston, who is always there on location, tells me are the easy part. "You've done all your hard work leading up to it. Filming isn't so difficult." Challenges await the film crew from the outset, though, since they have to lug their heavy – and fragile – camera equipment underground (unless they're at Charing Cross, where it can be carted in via train). "They need to bring all of the equipment down the stairs, thus not putting it on the escalators and damaging them," Reston explains. "The stairs are a bone of contention at Aldwych.

You always hear crews grumble, 'We don't want to work there because it's 160 stairs down!' A lot of the time these days they employ muscle to come in and do it for them." Her duties mostly boil down to protecting the stations and the crews. When a scene necessitates that actors go on the track, for example, TfL staff switch off the current and have safety experts on hand to assist ("People are frightened of being on the track and I don't blame them!").

Sometimes, a film's action takes place on platforms, down corridors, up escalators; other times, live trains are used, allowing characters to interact within a moving Tube carriage (the driver's cabs are out of bounds for shoots, though). Anyone who travels on the Underground is all too aware of the sustained, high-pitched mechanical screech the trains make when they're in motion; I know I've seen many commuters grimace and plug their ears to drown out the din. How do sound engineers record dialogue under these conditions? "The trains never pick up enough speed, so it's not really an issue," Reston explains. "I'll tell you what's *more* of an issue... the humming of the machinery. I remember doing *Sliding Doors*, and the sound man really didn't like the noise of the train engine. Sound men always ask us to switch it off, but we can't. They work around it. They can work around anything. They say they can't, but they really can."

The biggest job the TfL Film Office has worked on to date is, unsurprisingly, *Skyfall*. For Daniel Craig's second outing as James Bond, 007 pursues Javier Bardem's villain through a crowded Tube station, sliding down an escalator to catch him in an adrenaline-pumping action sequence that ends with a spectacular train crash. "Obviously we wouldn't let them crash a train!" Reston assures me. "They built that and we went along to Pinewood Studios to see it." All told, the project – which shot at Charing Cross with more than 450 cast and crew members over several weeks – amounted to almost a year's work. "They built this huge escalator rig connected to a sledge that they had to winch up, so the director of photography Roger Deakins would go down at the same time as Daniel Craig and Javier Bardem. No one's done it previously and no one's done it since."

After shooting wraps on the Underground, the film office takes a step back, while TfL's partnerships team reaches out to the production to see if they'd be willing to share their Tube experiences on the brand's social media channels. The romantic drama *All of Us Strangers*, which includes a scene where Paul Mescal and Andrew Scott look moody and melancholy on the Waterloo and City Line at Bank, took full advantage of this promotional opportunity. Scott told a charming anecdote about how he likes to sketch other passengers on the Underground for a TfL Instagram reel, and Mescal ranked his top three Tube Lines. I cheekily venture to Reston that Mescal's number-one choice – the branching, shrieking hellscape of the Northern Line – is categorically wrong. "Oh, that's subjective, that's subjective!" she says diplomatically between laughter. Does Reston have a particular favourite? "One of my favourite stations is Mornington Crescent. We did a Simply Red video there many, many years ago and it was a really nice job."

My own favourite stations, more than the ones with wide-carriage, air-conditioned trains (looking at you,

Metropolitan Line!), are those with a proper sense of character. Despite accusations that TfL passengers stare dead-eyed into the void, I love seeing Baker Street with its silhouetted, pipe-smoking Sherlock Holmeses lining the platform; Southwark with its funky, glass-panelled roof. London is a city that has been catalogued so extensively on film that the cinematic echoes are impossible to ignore. Navigating the Underground – even when commuting, even when running late – never fails to make me feel like a lady in a movie. •

LONDON UNDERGROUND

01 UNDERGROUND

1928   dir. Anthony Asquith

Fascinating time capsule, about a love triangle that takes place on and around the tube. There's a lovely montage of Waterloo.

02 MAN HUNT

1941   dir. Fritz Lang

Fritz Lang thriller (with Nazis!) set mostly in London – notable for its climatic chase scene through the Underground.

03 THE YELLOW BALLOON

1953   dir. J. Lee Thompson

A bomb-damaged tube station marks a major scene in this post-WWII drama, set amdist the rubble of the Blitz.

04 PICCADILLY THIRD STOP

1960   dir. Wolf Rilla

Little-seen British heist thriller about a plot to nab a large sum of money via the London Underground.

05 QUATERMASS AND THE PIT

1967   dir. Roy Ward Baker

A rail expansion unleashes an alien force at the fictional Hobbs End tube station. Shot at Elstree Studios.

06 DEATH LINE

1972   dir. Gary Sherman

Horror about weird stuff going on between Holborn and Russell Square stations. Hint: it's cannibals!

07 AN AMERICAN WEREWOLF IN LONDON

1981   dir. John Landis

A hairy beast hunts our hero through the eerily empty labyrinth of Tottenham Court Road station.

08 SLIDING DOORS

1998   dir. Peter Howitt

Two versions of life play out in parallel after Gwyneth Paltrow makes or misses her Tube connection.

09 CREEP

2004   dir. Christopher Smith

Miss the last Tube home and there will be terrible consequences – in itself a riff on 1972's *Death Line*.

10 SKYFALL

2012   dir. Sam Mendes

An explosive start in Vauxhall. Later, Bond hitches a ride at Charing Cross station (geography wonky).

SPIRITS OF THE BLITZ

BY LILLIAN CRAWFORD

Delving into the BFI archives prompts questions about how the cinema of the past – namely the works of Ealing and Powell and Pressburger – works to preserve prior generations

E ver since I was a child, I dreamed of exploring the archives of the British Film Institute. As such, I selected Ealing Studios – home to British classics like *Kind Hearts and Coronets*, *The Man in the White Suit*, and *The Lavender Hill Mob* – as the focus of my undergraduate dissertation, a decision which opened the door to a treasure trove of behind-the-scenes material, including Ealing producer Michael Balcon's personal papers and extensive publicity archives.

One interesting discovery came as I was reading the first page of the original shooting script for the 1955 black comedy *The Ladykillers*, written by William Rose. I noticed that the establishing description of the opening scene differed from the opening in the finished film:

"Directly below is Mum's two-storey Victorian house. Neighbouring buildings have suffered bomb damage and are uninhabited and Mum's house has clearly been damaged, because its walls on one side are supported by massive wooden struts. It looks lopsided, and yet its roofs and chimneys have such character that the cottage itself has a comic charm."

"Mum" is Mrs. Wilberforce (or "Louisa Alexandra Wilberforce," to give her full name). Played by Katie Johnson, this "small, slight, delicately-made and prettily-preserved" old lady stands for Britain, her name blending the royal and the political as to conjure great patriotic images of Victoriana. As in the script, the opening shot of *The Ladykillers* does show Mrs. Wilberforce's house, although there's one major difference in the film – the houses lining the road leading to her own are intact and appear completely free from bomb damage. But the original outline for the set-up better mirrors the characterisation of Mrs. Wilberforce as a bastion of a former England – the England which existed before the Second World War, and long before the Blitz. To show the oldest house on the street still standing while newer ones had fallen under the hellfire of the Luftwaffe would convey a sense of survival. Though this approach was likely cut for budgetary reasons, I was intrigued by the metaphor as originally intended by Rose.

The films of Ealing Studios, under the auspices of producer Michael Balcon, were often made from a position of personal experience and interests. It is a peculiarly British outlook (stiff upper lips, keeping calm and carrying on), relying on audiences with the same nostalgia and politics as the filmmakers themselves. Balcon himself described his team of directors and writers as "middle-class people brought up with middle-class backgrounds," although when the General Election of 1945 came and Britain faced the need for reconstruction, they voted Labour for the first time. "This," he said, "was our mild revolution."

The phrase recalls David Niven as Squadron Leader Peter Carter describing himself as "Conservative by nature, Labour by experience" as his Lancaster bomber is about to crash at the beginning of Powell and Pressburger's 1946 classic *A Matter of Life and Death*. Like Michael Powell, I grew up in Kent, although my heritage on my father's side is based in South London. I was raised in this in-between space, the working-class London roots of my father's mother

(Nan), and the more middle-class "Garden of England" of my mother's parents (Grandma and Grandad). Like the films of Ealing and Powell and Pressburger, these geographical backgrounds formed a melting pot of Conservative and Labour sensibilities.

All three of my surviving grandparents were children during the Second World War. I have often heard them talk of the post-war years when Britain was changing through Clement Attlee's government and back to Winston Churchill in October 1951, sitting in my Nan's maisonette on the outskirts of London or in the large garden of Grandma and Grandad's Kentish mock-Tudor house. To see them now, still in the same place but years older, they remind me of Mrs. Wilberforce – living, breathing embodiments of the past and its moralities.

The first Ealing film I saw as a child was the 1951 comedy *The Lavender Hill Mob*, a caper set in Battersea in which Alec Guinness and Stanley Holloway attempt to steal and smuggle gold bullion by disguising it as model Eiffel Towers. I quickly fell in love with Ealing, and watched the films (on "the telly") with my Nan whenever I went to stay with her. *The Ladykillers* made an even greater impression. I relished the blackness of the comedy as Guinness and his cronies tried to murder Mrs. Wilberforce after she discovered their plot to steal a case of money. Her endless nattering, chintz décor, baffling superstitions, and isolated contentment all felt very close to home.

If Nan was Ealing, Grandma was Powell and Pressburger – films about art, music, Technicolor. She introduced me to classical music, opera, and ballet as well as the films of

Pier Paolo Pasolini and Derek Jarman. I became especially enamoured with Powell and Pressburger. 1948's *The Red Shoes*, a film which left the Second World War out of its sensational dance world, was a particular favourite. As Powell wrote in 1986, "we had been told for ten years to go out and die for freedom and democracy [...] and now that the war was over, *The Red Shoes* told us to go and die for art."

Yet the war left its mark on Powell and Pressburger too. In 1944's *A Canterbury Tale*, Alison Smith (Sheila Sim) asks a lady for directions, saying she has not been in the city since 1940 and cannot find her way since so many buildings have been destroyed. "It is an awful mess, I don't blame you for not knowing where you are. But you get a very good view of the Cathedral now." Like Mrs. Wilberforce, Canterbury Cathedral towers over the war-torn streets, unyielding, and yet the damage done to Britain is apparent. Powell and Pressburger's previous film, *The Life and Death of Colonel Blimp*, ends with Clive Wynne-Candy (Roger Livesey), the "Colonel Blimp" figure of the title, standing by the remains of his bombed-out house in London, now an emergency water tank.

The charm of Ealing Studios, and Powell and Pressburger, has always been the insight they've provided into the England of my grandparents' childhoods. As they get older, this connection has only strengthened and watching these films fills me with anemoia – a nostalgia for a past that I never experienced myself. When I see films about evacuees and the bombing of London and Kent, I think of my grandparents and the dangers they faced, how they too were evacuated, and the lives they and their families rebuilt after the war. Despite not having been raised in London myself, I would feel connected to its landscape through my grandparents' stories and the films they shared with me.

One of my favourite anecdotes that my Grandad repeated during my childhood was about an unexploded bomb discovered on his street. It is always a delight to listen to Grandad's stories, all told countless times until – occasionally – a new one emerges, his eyes lighting up as he relives the moment, even as his memory has been failing. When he tells this particular story, Grandad recalls the plank used to climb across the pit containing the bomb, and how it had to be safely defused. It comes to mind when I watch Powell and Pressburger's *The Small Back Room* from 1949, which features an intense climax during which David Farrar must defuse a Nazi mine on Chesil Beach, and Ealing's 1949 *Passport to Pimlico*, in which an unexploded bomb goes off suddenly to reveal long-buried treasure.

In *Passport to Pimlico*, Arthur Pemberton (Stanley Holloway) hopes to turn a bombsite in South London into a playground for children. The plans are scuppered after the bomb explodes and a manuscript found in the underground cellar reveals that Pimlico still belongs to the Duchy of Burgundy. The film captures the essence of working-class British culture – as the populace heads into lockdown, no longer British citizens, they band together to sing songs like "Roll Out the Barrel" at the local pub. When Connie Pemberton (Betty Warren) is questioned about being English, she says, "We always were English, and we'll always be English, and it's just because we are English that we're sticking up for our right to be Burgundians!"

It is this communal obstinacy that Ealing films captured so beautifully, keeping calm and carrying on in peacetime, just as they did in war. In his 1981 book *Forever Ealing*, George Perry reflects on his 1949 diary:

> *"The war had been over for four years, but everyone was still obliged to have identity cards and ration books. Britain's streets still bore the gaping evidence of bombing, new building was strictly controlled, and even the most modest improvement to one's home required a building permit."*

Grandad's story about the unexploded bomb recalls a time when he and other children happily played on bomb sites. The first "Ealing comedy," 1947's *Hue and Cry*, opens with the camera moving from a long shot of the London skyline, littered with cranes, to the street on which young Joe Kirby (Harry Fowler) lives, his home one of few still standing. Kirby and his friends imitate dogfights amongst the rubble, now two years after Ernest Bevin had promised "five million homes in quick time" and Stafford Cripps boasted that the housing problem would be solved "in a fortnight" during the 1945 election. It was a gross understatement, and Bevin's successor, Aneurin Bevan, had to plan for a country with 700,000 fewer houses than there had been in 1939.

But there was hope for my grandparents' generation. I picture my Nan and Grandma as the title girl in Ealing's *Mandy*, from 1952, born of but not fully conscious of the nature of war. In that film, *Mandy*'s prospects are doubted by others due to her having been born deaf and unable to speak. Her parents protect her in their home, which backs onto a courtyard, with a bomb-damaged wall separating the space from a wider wasteland – the shattered London landscape left by the Blitz. At first, Mandy may only exist in the in-between space of the courtyard, but as she is helped at a specialist school for the deaf, she ventures out into the bombsite to play with the other children. Where Mandy's situation might seem bleak or without hope, the film shows that change and prosperity are on the horizon.

Today my grandparents resemble Mrs. Wilberforce more than Joe Kirby or Mandy, but their stories anchor the post-war films of Ealing and Powell and Pressburger in reality. They transform these films from mere stage depictions of the past into something more personal and emotionally resonant.

And now I, too, live in London and chuckle to myself every time I pass through Pimlico and think of the "Burgundians" storming onto the Underground to check the commuters' passports. I look for the sites where new homes and offices have been built, but I also visit Ealing Studios and see its buildings still standing like Mrs. Wilberforce's house does at the start of *The Ladykillers*. Just as Alison Smith can still hear the pilgrims on the road in *A Canterbury Tale*, the past continues to exist in the spaces and streets around us. Even when my grandparents are gone, it comforts me to know that the London of their childhood is preserved, forever, in film. •

EALING'S LONDON

01 THE BLACK SHEEP OF WHITEHALL

1942   dir. Basil Dearden, Will Hay

A professor tries to uncover a Nazi plot to disrupt a trade treaty – complicated comedy with a standout Will Hay.

02 IT ALWAYS RAINS ON SUNDAY

1947   dir. Robert Hamer

Set over a single day in Bethnal Green, as locals search for an escaped criminal – as poignant as it is thrilling.

03 HUE AND CRY

1947   dir. Charles Crichton

Kids uncover a criminal plot in the vibrant streets of London's East End, blending youthful adventure with mystery.

04 PASSPORT TO PIMLICO

1949   dir. Basil Dearden

A spirited romp set in post-war London, as a section of Pimlico is declared to be part of the state of Burgundy.

05 A RUN FOR YOUR MONEY

1949   dir. Charles Frend

Comedy about two Welsh miners who win a competition and travel to London, only to wind up battling the locals.

06 THE BLUE LAMP

1950   dir. Basil Dearden

A cop hunts a cop-killer in post-war Paddington, named for the blue lamps that once hung outside police stations.

07 POOL OF LONDON

1951   dir. Basil Dearden

Docklands-set noir-thriller from the great Basil Dearden, with nice location work in the titular Pool of London.

08 THE LAVENDER HILL MOB

1951   dir. Charles Crichton

Two mobsters plot to hijack a van filled with gold bullion in this Battersea-set comedy, with shades of Hitchcock.

09 THE LADYKILLERS

1955   dir. Alexander Mackendrick

Five criminals (including Alec Guinness) pose as a string quartet while planning a heist in King's Cross.

10 NOWHERE TO GO

1958   dir. Seth Holt

Tense noir about a London con-man who takes one risk too far; Holt called it "the least Ealing film ever made."

LETTER TO MY CINEMA SOULMATE

BY JASMINE VALENTINE

The vibrant cinema screens of London are more than just places to watch movies; they can also set the stage for new-found friendships built on film adoration

Dearest C.S.,

It was no chance encounter. You were waiting for me there, Aperol Spritz in hand, in the basement bar of the Curzon Soho, that glowing emblem of movie love wedged between the theatres and restaurants lining Shaftesbury Avenue.

After months of chatting online, not to mention countless just-missed meetings, I decided to take the plunge and gatecrash your solo night out – a trip to see Celine Sciamma's *Portrait of a Lady on Fire*, a film of sapphic yearning set on a remote island in the region of Brittany.

In Screen 1, we bonded over the lustful distance that Marianne (Noémie Merlant) and Héloïse (Adèle Haenel) held between them. Laughed as they rubbed herbs and hallucinogens into their armpits. And, watching them as they began to lose their own inhibitions, worked past the inevitable weirdness of finally meeting somebody in person who you'd only ever connected with through a phone screen.

I remember it vividly, of course, because meeting your Cinema Soulmate isn't something that happens every day. Or maybe ever.

Each time we – to paraphrase *Sunset Boulevard*'s ageing Hollywood recluse Norma Desmond – find ourselves sat among all those wonderful people in the dark, there's potential for a connection with a stranger. Because that is what cinema is about: we commit to the idea of engaging with a world outside our own, even if we do so wordlessly. You bask in the glow of the big screen with countless strangers, and if you're lucky, you come away having felt a special energy in the room. Fear, joy, sadness, lust. Sometimes, you might even become friends.

When I look back on what we have now, I think ours is a friendship that truly could have only been orchestrated by London. After all, in London, there is a place for everyone. Forget the myth about never engaging with somebody on the Underground; I believe a new connection is waiting around every corner for those who are willing to look.

A mix of varied souls under any one screen is, therefore, to be expected, whether you're taking in a blockbuster at the Peckhamplex or an arthouse classic at the ICA. The lawyer who rushes straight from work to catch Bill Nighy's latest drama on the back of her membership. The tourist who has a plane to catch, but is risking it anyway, just so they can say they saw a movie in one of the city's iconic picturehouses. The old couple who have been coming to the same cinema for years, and always make sure to book the exact same seats (A23 and A24, right near the front).

So there we were – two strangers from totally different generations, backgrounds, worlds, sensing that something significant was afoot. Do you remember? Amidst the crowd of film buffs, waiting patiently for their screens to open, our first conversation flowed with ease and without hesitation.

I'd had the luck of meeting you, my Cinema Soulmate, in the depths of the internet, where we'd quickly bonded over our ever-growing back catalogue of beloved favourites and yet-to-sees. True, it was our local cinemas that first brought us together and sparked a conversation, neither of us originally from the city where we'd eventually spend most of our time together. Live recordings of National Theatre productions played out in ill-equipped arts centres, with texts batted back and forth to assess what might have transpired if we'd had actually been in the same room. It was fun, but as with a formidable pen pal, that kind of thing can only get you so far.

London bridged the gap, the city's cinemas more than willing to play perfect host as we tried to figure out whether this thing could actually work in real life. Céline Sciamma might have set us on the right path during that platonic first date, but just as much as we were hooked on each other, we were infatuated with the fast-paced, theatrical city of our encounters. Almost four years later, an abundance of London cinema venues have played a small yet incredibly significant role in shaping the most important friendship in my life – and for that, I must give my thanks.

For me, a humble cinema attendee and two-time membership holder, London is inextricably tied to its love of film, and the countless opportunities it offers to the willing cinephile. Where else could I be sat with friends in their 20s, 30s, 40s, and 50s, taking in the quiet revelations of Yasujirō Ozu, the kitschy camp and gore of Dario Argento, the gentle, dorky humour of Greta Gerwig? All credit to the multiplexes, but these films aren't pushed by chains whose goal is to upsell hot dogs and plastic cups – there's programmed intention behind them, real affection for the material. London's cinemas ask us to delve deeper — not just in ourselves, but the people who we choose to sit and absorb the movies alongside.

After our first meet proved a hit, it made sense for London to play host to our fledgling friendship going forward: meals out, creative immersions, drinking until we dropped (this city, we discovered, was more than willing to oblige). In less than two hours, we could go from leading our separate lives to being ensconced in an ongoing narrative, creating memories off the back of other people's art – films, seemingly, created just for us.

We moved from the confines of the Curzon to the exquisite time capsule that is the Prince Charles Cinema, allowing me to experience one of your most revered films: David Lynch's *Mulholland Drive*. Sometimes, the only way to strengthen a bond is to get straight to the heart of what makes the other person tick. The seductively confusing stylings of Lynch, coupled with the sapphic overtures (and furiously sad wanks), opened the floodgates for new conversations and deeper understanding. Emotion, as you know, isn't something that comes naturally to me. When you're raised in a household that prioritises proactive solutions over proper (and healthy) emoting, finding ways to connect on a deeper level feels like a never-ending uphill climb. I have no doubt in my mind that it was the moments we shared that allowed internal barriers to break for the first time in my life.

It's probably not something I should admit, as someone who makes a living off the back of writing about TV and films, but London was, until fairly recently, less on my radar than you might expect. But those day trips to the city with my parents, when I was young, were about as close as you could get to receiving manna from heaven. I walked, wide-eyed, taking in the wider cultural scene, finally feeling free of the glass ceiling. In London, anything seemed possible.

At 28, London is still where I retreat to when I want alone time, or to be heard in a way that properly correlates with how I feel on the inside – strange, perhaps, considering how London is often viewed as the very opposite of a sanctuary.

But with you, my Cinema Soulmate, London is the playground where anything goes. It's where we saw *Spirited Away* on the big screen for the first time – and in its original Japanese subtitling. From there, we graced Regent Street to find ourselves immersed in the height of *Barbie* hype, knowing that the only way to take in the size of Greta Gerwig's vision was to be right there together, in the heart of the city. Armed with sickly sweet cocktails and hula wreaths presented at the door, London made a point of highlighting the film's fuchsia chaos.

We've cried at the tender, queer tapestry of *Blue Jean* in the heart of the BFI Southbank, clinging to words of hope and inspiration from its director and cast. Going beyond the screen into matters that affect our personal lives, London sets a stage for filmic experiences that money can only superficially buy a ticket to. The city's unique blend of architecture, programming, community, and understanding makes for an artistic fondue. We wouldn't shift, even if you tried to move us. No, our friendship doesn't depend on it. But without it, the lights may dim a little.

On the surface, there's no way any of this should work. Through it all, you have been the friend I've always wanted. You speak to me through film, whether that's in choosing what we watch, debriefing our latest viewing in way too much detail, or merely sitting in silence in those special moments afterwards, taking it all in. Being together in those

London screening rooms gives me what I've always felt I lacked: support, understanding, and patience – right there, in the seat next to me. When there aren't enough words to tell you what you mean to me, or I find communication fails, those wonderful moments spent in the dark seem to do all the talking on my behalf.

So, to you, my Cinema Soulmate, to whom I write this meandering love letter: I couldn't do it without you. And to London, the third wheel in our wondrous twosome, a city of unrelenting empathy and artistic endeavour, who beckons me into the dark – and hopefully into a comfortable seat – to be moved, awed, and transformed, time and time again. The city, and you. Always with you. These parts of me exist, intertwined, forever connected as part of the same whole. Together, we're lucky to have it all. •

LONDON FRIENDSHIPS

01 THE FALLEN IDOL

1948   dir. Carol Reed

A young boy witnesses what he thinks is a murder by the butler he looks up to; Pauline Kael called it a "polite thriller."

02 84 CHARING CROSS ROAD

1987   dir. David Jones

Bookshop magic on London's Charing Cross Road as Anthony Hopkins and Anne Bancroft become pen pals across the pond.

03 FOUR WEDDINGS AND A FUNERAL

1994   dir. Mike Newell

Hugh Grant bumbles his way through London's grand churches, the South Bank, and Smithfield Market.

04 ME WITHOUT YOU

2001   dir. Sandra Goldbacher

Best friends from the suburbs navigate love and loss in '70s London; Michelle Williams and Anna Friel co-star.

05 BEND IT LIKE BECKHAM

2002   dir. Gurinder Chadha

Football dreams collide with cultural traditions in Hounslow. Eyes peeled for the David Beckham cameo (sort of).

06 MRS. PALFREY AT THE CLAREMONT

2005   dir. Dan Ireland

Lo-fi but sweet tale set in a ramshackle London hotel, where an elderly widow (Joan Plowright) befriends a writer.

07 SOMERS TOWN

2008   dir. Shane Meadows

King's Cross transformation meets Camden grit in this Eurostar-funded gem about two unlikely young friends.

08 GINGER & ROSA

2012   dir. Sally Potter

Story of two friends (Elle Fanning and Alice Englert) growing up in a wonderful recreation of '60s London.

09 THE LADY IN THE VAN

2015   dir. Nicholas Hytner

Playwright Alan Bennett bonds with an eccentric old woman (Maggie Smith) who lives on his Camden driveway.

10 ROCKS

2019   dir. Sarah Gavron

Slice of life drama about a Black British girl in Hackey raising her sister; the friendships feel genuinely lived-in.

FOUR YEARS

BY JACK BLACKWELL

Four years, 379 reviews... but how was London represented on the big screen during a period of cultural uncertainty and global unease?

For four years, I had the pleasure of reviewing new releases for WeLoveCinema, week in, week out. Throughout this period, I tackled a diverse array of films, contributing a total of 379 reviews between 2019 and 2023. My journey began with a review of the poignant Chinese drama *So Long, My Son* and concluded with an exploration of Nepal's past, present, and future in the documentary *Baato*. These writings covered everything from foreign-language festival favorites and blockbusters to indie gems and digital-only releases, with countless hours spent in cinemas and screening rooms throughout the capital.

I can map out my memories of these weeks through those 379 reviews; how I felt when certain films debuted in cinemas, screenings drawing me back to what was happening in the world at the time. The Irish crime drama Calm With Horses, for example, sticks with me as a harbinger of the looming COVID pandemic. It was 13 March 2020, ten days before we were placed under lockdown, and the only other person in the theatre was an older gentleman who sat as far from me as possible, darting over distrustful glances at having to share the same air. But there were also real events, too – for all that you have to navigate a piss-covered maze in the middle of Waterloo to get there, going to the BFI IMAX to see Oppenheimer on the fabled "Barbenheimer" opening night was an experience like no other.

WeLoveCinema's ethos of covering smaller films as well as the mainstream releases led me to all kinds of neighbourhoods, granting me a wider view of not just

London's cinemas, but of the city itself. My beloved local, the Clapham Picturehouse, is one such lovely spot – a cinema that feels like a warm, rural theatre dropped mysteriously into Zone 2 – and you can get a café lunch and a pint there, making it my go-to (technically, my absolute local is the Streatham Odeon, but that, like most Odeons, is a grim and sticky place cursed with shameful projection). Some screenings, however, necessitated a pilgrimage to as far afield as Chiswick or Hackney, or to cinemas as singular and baffling as the Curzon in Camden (where tiny screens are nestled under railway arches, the films often accompanied by a slight rumble every eight or so minutes). Having lived in three places across a roughly one-and-a-half-mile radius in South West London over the last six years, these cinematic trips reminded me that I live in one of the world's most important and varied capitals, and not just in the slightly insular village of Balham and Clapham.

It's in this spirit of rediscovery that I found myself wondering how London itself had been represented through films released across the four years I worked as a film critic for WeLoveCinema. The late 90s and early noughties had largely painted the capital as a place for posh and pained singles to find love, as in *Sliding Doors, Notting Hill, Bridget Jones' Diary* and many more – and into the late noughties and early 2010s, London became more a backdrop for bombastic plots in disaster, action, and dystopian cinema. Did films set in London between 2019 and 2023 manage to eke out their own cohesive identity – and what did any of it manage to say about the state of things?

As is ever the case with London, the answer is complicated.

What's initially obvious is a renewed vigour for this country's apparently never-ending relationship with nostalgia; maybe because our situation in these past four years felt so strange, filmmakers turned to the London of the past. Not all these efforts emerged as cosy distractions. One that did was 2022's *The Duke*, Roger Michell's final narrative feature film, which served as the perfect coda to a warm, witty, and varied career that was tragically cut short. Based on a larger-than-life true story, *The Duke* follows Kempton Bunton (Jim Broadbent), a cabbie who, in 1961, stole the Francisco de Goya portrait of the Duke of Wellington from London's National Gallery in an act of protest against the UK government paying £140,000 to keep it in the country instead of spending that money on vulnerable people. It was quick of wit and fleet of foot, the kind of film custom-built for family viewing on a Sunday night, lifting you into the next week with a wink and a smile. Other releases made in this vein tried to tap into that uncomplicatedly crowd-pleasing style of British period fare. I also reviewed London-set films *The Electrical Life of Louis Wain*, *Enola Holmes*, *Operation Mincemeat*, *The Courier*, and *See How They Run* – perfectly watchable, if slightly middling efforts, crafted for those still eager to consume a cor, blimey! version of The Big Smoke, many designed to lure dads into cinemas for their twice-yearly outings. If it's starring Emma Thompson or Benedict Cumberbatch or Colin Firth, you can bet that a certain subset of the British public will dig deep into their pockets.

Other London-set films that aimed to tap into the nostalgia of noughties rom-coms fell hopelessly flat, however. One example of some of the worst London-set material to surface during these years was *Locked Down*, a wildly aggravating pandemic rom-com. Starring Chiwetel Ejiofor and Anne Hathaway, it sees a hateful couple have their break up stymied by the 2020 spring lockdown in the UK, forcing them to stay together in their spacious, three-storey London townhouse. From the off, the pair's "woe is me" shtick is insufferable as they flounce around their bright, sleek home, trying to avoid each other. On top of this, though, *Locked Down* could not have been worse suited to the time it was released; yes, it was a film about the pandemic made and released during the pandemic, but it treats COVID not as a direct threat to people's health, finances, and homes, but as a temporary stumbling block for unhappy rich people who are still in the midst of finding themselves – and stealing a $3 million diamond from London's Harrods department store. The appeal of an airy comedy about that then-current crisis was, to say the least, severely limited.

Yet more proof of bumbling, London-set rom-coms losing their verve was the excruciating *What's Love Got to Do with It?*, in which unlucky-in-love documentarian Zoe (Lily James) is surprised to learn that her childhood neighbour Kazim (Shazad Latif) has decided he wants to settle down in a marriage orchestrated by his patient but traditional Pakistani parents. Generic in its culture-clash drama, embarrassing in its comedy, and unconvincing as a romance, *What's Love Got to Do With It?* is frequently brought low by shabby editing, boring visuals, and some of the most distracting Bad London Geography in recent memory – my breaking point with the whole endeavour was a moment in which Zoe steps out of a Mayfair function for some air and ends up, somehow, on the Southbank. This is a film that is just dying to emulate those classic Richard Curtis London rom-coms, but it can't even get the basics of the city it's set in right.

Where new and exciting talent did emerge, however, was through the diverse perspectives brought by a number of debut filmmakers. After suffering through *What's Love Got To Do With It?*, what a joyous balm it was to watch a London rom-com that actually loves London: Raine Allen-Miller's wonderful debut film *Rye Lane* commits fully to its location, forming the backbone of just why this Peckham and Brixton-set spin on the *Before Sunrise* format feels just so wonderful, where the leads have the kind of chemistry that most rom-coms would kill for. *Rye Lane* has no interest in the typically grey Serious London colour palette of shows like *Industry* or *Top Boy*, instead harking back to the sunny warmth of classic Richard Curtis (though the cast here is a lot more realistically diverse than you'd see in the likes of *Notting Hill*). Pinks, blues, greens, and yellows fill the screen, while dream sequences and flashbacks are pulled off with a great sense of ambition and flair, the two leads' recollections turning their lives into a stage show in which they get to be the stars.

There was much to love about Reggie Yates' feature directorial debut *Pirates*, too, a short and sharp comedy set over the course of roughly nine hours which doubles as an ode to late '90s North London, a coming-of-age tale set amongst its director's old stomping grounds. You will certainly get more enjoyment out of *Pirates* if you live or have lived in London yourself, as Yates draws a lot of comedic mileage out of the often insurmountable divide between the north and south sides of the river; with the abundance of inside jokes, the dialogue really does feel like it's coming from a years-long friendship, but never at the expense of the audience – and credit must be given to the casting team for finding three young Londoners with such great chemistry in Elliot Edusah, Reda Elazouar, and Jordan Peters.

Elsewhere, in Dionne Edwards' *Pretty Red Dress*, set predominantly in the boroughs of Croydon and Bromley, we got a stylish look at Black masculinity, sexuality, and gender norms that balanced a witty warmth with something more confrontational. It subversively examined how families can act as a repressive microcosm of a heteronormative society without even realising it.

And in Bassam Tariq's *Mogul Mowgli* – ignoring the heavy-handed metaphor that drives the plot – we were gifted with a keenly observed film about social and cultural dilemmas unfolding in the capital. It stars Riz Ahmed as Zed, a British rapper on the cusp of breaking into stardom in America with his passionate and powerful lyrics about his Pakistani origins, even though he's taken pains to distance himself from his familial roots – he bristles at being called his real name, Zaheer, and it transpires that he hasn't seen his parents in two years. With a make-or-break tour of Europe on the horizon, Zed returns home to London for a week of reunions before the gigs start. *Mogul Mowgli* interrogates the various ways in which immigrants try to integrate with British society whilst keeping their own identities alive, and how impossible this push-pull dynamic can feel; there are some deeply cathartic moments whenever Zed briefly finds the balance that keeps both his family and career on side.

The great Daniel Kaluuya switched roles from in front of to behind the camera to direct his feature debut *The Kitchen*, a solid dystopian social drama co-directed with Kibwe Tavares, which was at its best when showing London through Kaluuya's eyes as a young, socially conscious Black creative (not to mention die-hard Arsenal fan). The film focuses on a man living in the eponymous "Kitchen," a sprawling estate that stands as the last publicly-owned residential space in London while the rest of the city has seemingly been entirely taken over by a property company called Buena Vida. In what is probably the film's most interesting touch, though, our protagonist (*Top Boy*'s Kano) has no desire to protect the Kitchen, no pride in its community spirit, and is instead desperate to get on the Buena Vida property ladder. It's a refreshingly unsentimental look at the limits of local pride and tradition; and yes, a lot of *The Kitchen* could absolutely take place in modern London, which is certainly the point, even if it's a point that leaves the film rather in conflict with itself.

Perhaps the most impressive of all these debuts, though, was Remi Weekes' *His House*, a disturbing account of the London refugee experience, whereby a married couple flee the war in South Sudan and find refuge in the city, housed in a nondescript area somewhere in a low-income neighbourhood. Their relief at finding a new home is swiftly replaced by terror, however, as a malevolent spirit living in the walls begins to torment them. The spirit's constant assertions that the pair need to return home make it an effective avatar of Hostile Environment Britain, obsessed with getting rid of migrants no matter how vile the consequences. Weekes does a fantastic job of making the streets and alleys of suburban London feel as alien to the audience as they do to his characters, while avoiding the clichés one might expect from a refugee drama.

It's refreshing, and heartening, then, to see the most compelling portrayals of London emerging from a new cohort of cinematic voices. For all the cosy, throwback flicks starring LAMDA grads with Harrow schooling, there was a debut filmmaker taking strides to rip up the rulebook and redefine the city on screen, capturing London as it truly is – sometimes romantic, frequently harsh, yet always irresistible thanks to the endless contradictions. •

UNDERSEEN LONDON GEMS

01 THE L-SHAPED ROOM

1962   dir. Bryan Forbes

London opens its arms to a pregnant single Frenchwoman, who finds unexpected support in a boarding house.

02 WEST 11

1963   dir. Michael Winner

A criminal with a penchant for jazz (what's better than that?) contemplates murder in this Michael Winner gem.

03 THE SMALL WORLD OF SAMMY LEE

1963   dir. Ken Hughes

A strip club host races to escape thugs in this gritty, fast-paced '60s thriller shot in the sleazy streets of Soho.

04 THE NANNY

1965   dir. Seth Holt

Deliciously unhinged psycho-biddy Hammer Horror starring Bette Davis as the nanny from hell – a British *Baby Jane*.

05 BETRAYAL

1983   dir. David Jones

Jeremy Irons is a cipher for playwright Harold Pinter in this extramarital love triangle, told in reverse.

06 MONA LISA

1986   dir. Neil Jordan

Ex-con Bob Hoskins falls for a sex worker in this subversive neo-noir about an unlikely romance. Shades of *Taxi Driver*.

07 LONDON KILLS ME

1991   dir. Hanif Kureishi

New shoes represent a better life for a drug user in Hanif Kureishi's underseen but underrated Notting Hill-set drama.

08 CLOSE MY EYES

1991   dir. Stephen Poliakoff

Docklands development, the AIDS crisis, and incest combine in a film where Clive Owen cuckolds Alan Rickman.

09 WONDERLAND

1999   dir. Michael Winterbottom

Sadcore musings of three sisters over Bonfire Night weekend – capturing the bright lights and ennui of London life.

10 THE MOTHER

2003   dir. Roger Michell

Handyman Daniel Craig engages in a bit of upstairs-downstairs with a lonely mother (Anne Reid) and her daughter.

The

End

YOU MOVE TO LONDON IN 2013 AND QUICKLY FIND YOURSELF SWEPT UP IN ITS ALLURE. EVEN WITH THE MOODY WEATHER, CLIMBING RENT PRICES, AND CONSTANT SMOKE AND TRAFFIC, YOU CAN'T HELP BUT TAKE COMFORT IN THE IDEA OF LONDON AS A PLACE WHERE ARTISTS THROUGHOUT HISTORY HAVE THRIVED, WHERE EVERY CORNER HAS BEEN CAPTURED ON CANVAS OR IMMORTALIZED IN FILM – OR IS WAITING TO BE.

You begin to feel at home, though one thing about London soon becomes apparent: navigating the city's thriving film scene is quite the challenge. Knowing what's showing, and where, feels like an endless game of catch-up. Missed opportunities like the Korean Film Festival, or that one-off screening of *Embrace of the Serpent*, leave you feeling like you're always behind the curve. And you are oblivious to the amazing venues outside of the usual multiplexes, like the Prince Charles and the BFI, let alone deeper cuts like the ICA, the Castle, or the Rio. What's the point of an amazing party if you don't know when or where it's happening?

And so the idea for WeLove-Cinema is born – to guide London's cine-curious to the screenings they didn't even know they were missing. You rally fellow film fanatics to the cause, quickly learning that a simple listings site won't suffice. With over 25,000 weekly showtimes (including regular and special screenings, previews, not to mention 3D and IMAX showings, too), 150 venues (from historical cinemas to one-night pop-up venues), and a database of over 15,000 films (and counting!), simplifying this chaos becomes a unified mission.

Liam codes, Dale handles marketing, Fedor takes care of the data, Tom works as editor, curating content and reviews from an extraordinary pool of talented, fiercely independent film critics. You have the pleasure of overseeing the entire production. Together, you spread your love for cinema and the capital, helping Londoners to make informed, cost-effective decisions on how to spend their evenings.

Seven wonderful years pass, marked by humble beginnings and triumphant milestones, from local screenings to our participation in star-studded international festivals like Cannes, Berlin, and Venice. What begins with a handful of friends visiting the site blossoms into over half a million weekly users.

Now, in a period of economic constraint, it's time to take a break. Yet, it's also a time to celebrate – a success story made possible by a wonderful, dedicated team, supportive venues, sensational writers, and a fantastic film-loving community.

To everyone involved – thank you. It's been an honour and a joy. Yes, we *still* love cinema, and this city, and here's the book to prove it. •

CONTRIBUTORS

TOM BARNARD served as the Editor of *WeLoveCinema* between 2019–2023. He has also written for the BFI. He lives in London and is currently working on a novel about AI.

JACK BLACKWELL is a London-based film writer who was *WeLoveCinema's* most published critic. He writes regularly at blackwellfilm.com and has also written for *One Room with a View*.

LILLIAN CRAWFORD is a freelance writer whose writing has appeared in *Little White Lies, Sight & Sound,* and *BBC Culture*. She also works as a programmer, and is currently completing a PhD on *Screen Two*.

RORY DOHERTY is a film critic based in Edinburgh, Scotland. He writes regularly for *Flicks, Vulture, Paste, GQ,* and *The A.V. Club*.

BEN FLANAGAN is a London-based film writer and the Editor-in-Chief of *Cinema Year Zero*. He has also written for *photogénie, Slant,* and *MUBI Notebook*.

STEPH GREEN is a London-born Greek Cypriot film critic who also works in the travel industry. She writes for publications including *The Guardian, BBC, Sight & Sound, Empire* and *IndieWire*.

ELLA KEMP is a writer, photographer, and broadcaster, and the London Editor of Letterboxd. Her writing has appeared in *Little White Lies, British GQ, IndieWire,* and *Sight & Sound*.

LEILA LATIF is a freelance film critic and broadcaster. She writes regularly for *The Guardian, IndieWire,* and *Sight & Sound,* and is the host of *Truth & Movies: A Little White Lies Podcast*.

MANUELA LAZIĆ is a French film critic, actor, director, and podcast host who lives in London. Her work has been featured in *The Ringer, RogerEbert.com,* and *The Guardian*.

ANNA MCKIBBIN is an Irish-born film critic who now resides in London. Her work has appeared in *Paste, Little White Lies,* and *Vague Visages*.

CONTRIBUTORS

EMILY MASKELL is a freelance film critic, culture writer, and script reader based in London, who has written for *Little White Lies, BBC Culture, Vulture,* and *GQ.* She is the author of *Icons of Cinema: Baz Luhrmann.*

LILIA PAVIN-FRANKS is a film writer, programmer, and event producer focusing mainly on female-led and queer cinema. She currently works as an Event Coordinator at the BFI Southbank.

RAFA SALES ROSS is a Brazilian freelance film journalist and programmer who currently resides in Scotland. She has a Master's in Film and Visual Culture and has written for *Variety, BBC Culture,* and *Sight & Sound.*

HANNAH STRONG is the Digital Editor of *Little White Lies* magazine. Her freelance work has also appeared in *Vice, BBC Culture,* and *GQ.* Her first book, *Sofia Coppola: Forever Young,* was published in May 2022.

JASMINE VALENTINE is the Editor-in-Chief of *FILMHOUNDS Magazine* and a freelance entertainment journalist. She has also written for *Little White Lies, Total Film,* and *Radio Times.*

YASMIN OMAR is the Editor-in-Chief of the *Curzon Journal.* A member of the London Film Critics' Circle, she also writes for *Empire, Little White Lies,* and *Harper's Bazaar.*

SAVINA PETKOVA is a Bulgarian freelance culture writer based in London. She has a PhD in Film Studies from King's College London and has written for *MUBI Notebook* and *Little White Lies.*

ADAM SOLOMONS is a writer and film critic whose writing has appeared in *Little White Lies, IndieWire,* and *AwardsWatch.* He currently works as an Assistant Producer at Times Radio.

FEDOR TOT is a freelance film critic and curator specializing in Yugoslav and ex-Yugoslav cinema. He has written for *MUBI Notebook, Bright Wall/Dark Room,* and *Screen Slate.*

LAURA VENNING is a Crouch End-based freelance film critic who writes regularly for *Empire, Little White Lies,* and the *Curzon Journal.* She is currently working on a book about the films of Greta Gerwig.

CREDITS

BIG SMOKE,
BIG SCREEN

A WELOVECINEMA BOOK

Editor	Tom Barnard
Deputy Editor	Steph Green
Proofreaders	Fedor Tot, Dave Ferner
Designer	Rejane Dal Bello
Design Assistant	Elaine Miles
Managing Director	Juanjo Barreda

WELOVECINEMA WEBSITE TEAM

Founder and CEO	Juanjo Barreda
Editor	Tom Barnard
Developer	Liam Moody
Data Manager	Fedor Tot
Marketing Manager	Dale Edwards

CREDITS

THANKS TO OUR WELOVECINEMA WRITERS

Alasdair Bayman

Jack Blackwell

Cathy Brennan

Lex Briscuso

Kambole Campbell

Eddie Charles

Lillian Crawford

Rory Doherty

Rose Dymock

Ben Flanagan

Andrew Gaudion

Steph Green

Lyanna Hindley

Yasmine Kandil

Ella Kemp

Jack King

Jordan King

Leila Latif

Manuela Lazić

Barry Levitt

Jack Martin

Emily Maskell

Anna McKibbin

Mireia Mullor

Iana Murray

Yasmin Omar

Joseph Owen

Rahul Patel

Lilia Pavin-Franks

Savina Petkova

Rafa Sales Ross

Alistair Ryder

Ren Scateni

Adam Solomons

Hannah Strong

Xuanlin Tham

Millicent Thomas

Fedor Tot

Jasmine Valentine

Laura Venning

Billie Walker